Prince

Prince

A Life in Music

A Playlist History

Matthew Carcieri

iUniverse, Inc.
New York Lincoln Shanghai

Prince
A Life in Music

iUniverse, Inc.

For information address:
iUniverse, Inc.
2021 Pine Lake Road, Suite 100
Lincoln, NE 68512
www.iuniverse.com

ISBN: 0-595-32012-0

Printed in the United States of America

Thanks

to Kristin—for the music in my life

to my sisters—for joining me in the dance

to Sarah B.—for a ticket on the purple bus

FOREWORD

In 1958 the American Midwest gave birth to three of the greatest icons of pop music. Two of them—Madonna and Michael Jackson—would redefine pop culture through the sheer size of their ubiquitous stardom (and occasional notoriety). The third would reshape the course of pop with his relentless artistic rebellion and unparalleled musicianship.

Few artists have simultaneously scaled the split peaks of artistic and commercial success the way Prince has. For the better part of 25 years, his image and style have provoked and titillated pop culture. Marrying soul-stirring ideas on sex and salvation with innovative and inspired songwriting, he's generated worldwide sales of over 100 million records. Fusing rock, funk and R&B in one of the most successful crossover acts of all time, he set a record by scoring a Top 10 hit every year for 12 consecutive years.

He is arguably the most complete virtuoso in the history of music, and he's been anointed the best showman ever to hit the stage. He's an accomplished guitarist, bass player, pianist, beat master, lyricist, vocalist, engineer, producer and bandleader. He's rewritten the rules of creative enterprise and pulled off some perilous marketing stunts. He's launched more than a few minor stars and put his home city on the musical map. He's issued the longest new recording in history and filmed two of the best rock movies ever made.

Along the way, he's amassed an unprecedented catalog, almost single-handedly writing, performing and producing 100 albums worth of material since his debut. And that only counts the songs that have been released. It's reported that he's stashed away another 1,000 cuts in his famed vault.

His career has been a blaze of creativity, and because of him, there's a new standard in the music business—and a whole new set of rules.

In the year of his acclaimed comeback, *Prince: A Life in Music* celebrates the career of the most influential and prolific artist of our time. It tells the story of his storied career, and it recounts the tale through his songs. *Prince: A Life in Music* is a "playlist history"—a career retrospective organized around 50 tracks that describe Prince's eventful journey. Each song presents a chapter, and together, they assemble a soundtrack to a remarkable life.

For a talent as prolific as Prince, the music *is* his life, and his life is his music. It's only appropriate that the story be told through his songs.

So read along—and listen when you're able—to an inspiring human drama: the epic story of a musical warrior, a libertarian crusader who would fight at all cost so creativity would reign supreme.

TRACK LISTING

PRINCE:
A LIFE IN MUSIC

Playlist One: Lustful Ambition (1958-1982)

PRINCE:
A LIFE IN MUSIC

Playlist Two: Haughty Heights (1983-1986)

PRINCE:
A LIFE IN MUSIC

Playlist Three: Soulful Struggles (1987-1993)

PRINCE:
A LIFE IN MUSIC

Playlist Four: Independent Crusade (1994-2004)

PROLOGUE

"Na na, na na, na na, na na, BAT-MAN!"

A young boy watched with riveted fixation. This was one of his favorite shows.

"To the Batmobile," the Caped Crusader commanded. Like the battle cry of a holy warrior, his tone bespoke both the danger and the glory of his crusade.

The funky, black roadster roared off, speeding away with the heart of the young boy, drawing the little viewer deeper and deeper into the fantasy of the Dark Knight. It carried him to another dimension, a dreamy, Technicolor vision not all that far from reality.

Here was the story of an ordinary human being who, with a change of his costume, could enter a world of comic-book wonders. In the ashes of a childhood cut short by hardship, he'd found a burning self-purpose and created his own super powers. He embraced the darkness as an ally and turned his tortured soul into an agent for good. Working night after night in his solitary cave, he would prevail of his own determination and drive.

The little boy padded across the room to the piano that his father had left behind. Poking deliberately at the keys, the boy's fingers constructed a phrase: "Na na, na na, na na, na na, BAT-MAN!"

Playlist One: Lustful Ambition (1958-1982)

Track 1: "Games"

Whether it was for greatness or for ridicule and reclusion, the boy was certainly marked. He was born into a family of amateur musicians, and his father—an impassioned pianist who lived for his after-hour gigs with a jazz trio—gave his firstborn son his stage name: Prince Rogers Nelson.

As if a bizarro name—the mantle of a father's dreams—wasn't enough of a cross to bear, the young black child was also saddled with a strangely small stature.

In the gray Minneapolis suburb that was his home, life for a little black Prince often grew bitterly cold. His parents divorced when he was 10, and trouble at home sent the gentle, Afro-ed youngster bouncing between guardians throughout his adolescence. What came out of the wash in school was a quiet, withdrawn kid who found his happiness in the same place his father found it: alone at the piano.

The legend of Prince's youth tells of formative moments when the joy of music brightened the little lad's soul. One was getting carted by his dad to a James Brown show, where Prince was momentarily hoisted onto the stage. The other was a forbidden peak into one of his dad's own stage shows. The crowd's raucous affirmation for his father seemed to have made a lasting impression.

By age 13, Prince was living with a family from the Seventh-Day Adventist Church that was a centerpiece of the local black community. There he shared a basement bedroom with a close friend named André Anderson. Like Prince, André fancied himself a musician, and together, the two established a virtual training camp in their basement lair. They immersed themselves in the music of Carlos Santana, James Brown, Sly and the Family Stone and Jimi Hendrix and picked up every instrument they could get their hands on.

1

By high school, the pair had formed a band called Grand Central (later renamed Champagne when one of their musical idols—Larry Graham, the bassist for Sly and the Family Stone—created his Graham Central Station). The group played school dances and neighborhood parties. Before long, they were writing and performing their own material, and they evolved the band into a pretty serious operation with slick costumes: suede suits stitched with their zodiac signs. The quiet Prince who played lead guitar was a Gemini.

Prince had a distant relative who was a record producer and served as an early career mentor. Through him, Prince and André were enlisted for a small-label project in Minneapolis, a loose collection of session players called 94 East. (The recordings remained in the can and were later released against Prince's will after he'd hit it big.) One of Prince's earliest recordings on a professional studio project was "GAMES," a drawn-out jam that emphasized his disco-soul roots and the deep grooving that characterized his musical formation. These sessions revealed just how deftly the two friends could handle a jam, and Prince demonstrated the fruits of reclusive self-instruction by busting convincing performances on guitar, keyboards and drums. (André handled bass.)

The pint-sized black kid with a silly name and broken family had a lot to prove; and behind his shy, introverted eyes, a massive plot was beginning to form. With these early events, the rock gods offered music as a salvation, and Prince decided he would shoot straight for the stars. Frustrated by his size, Prince Rogers Nelson would be gigantic. Mocked for his unusual name, he would put it in lights. Disregarded at home, he would be loved by millions. Prince would be King.

From a very early age, Prince had a strong sense of destiny. All it took was self-discipline and lots of hard work. Putting the wheels in motion, he capitalized on his high school's top-notch music program and poured himself into music theory, stage band and an important course called "The Business of Music." Although he showed promise on the basketball court—where he was a highly skilled ball handler and a pivotal sixth man in spite of his size—Prince quit the high-school team and redoubled his efforts on guitar. Strict dedication became the order of the day. He took lead control of his and André's band, and when not running rehearsals, the Puritanical teenager was more interested in practicing an instrument than hanging out with friends or wasting himself on parties, drinking or drugs.

By the end of high school, Prince was ready to make his move. He doubled up on his credits—going to school for longer hours—and graduated six months early. On the eve of graduation, Prince confided to a classmate that he was about to be a star.

TRACK 2: "SOFT AND WET"

While still in high school, Prince brought his band into a local, eight-track production studio with hopes of cutting a record demo. Again, his individual skills stood out, and the owner of the studio, an entrepreneurial British transplant named Christopher Moon, pulled him aside with ideas for a partnership. They hatched a deal that gave Prince unlimited access to the rudimentary production setup in return for shared profits on any outcomes. The opportunity meant walking away from his band, and the star-struck teen didn't look back.

Prince spent most of his 18th year practically living in the studio. Holing up alone in the small facility, he often stayed there for entire weekends, catching some brief sleep on a couch. He spent months upon months learning to master the studio console and improving his dexterity on a growing list of instruments. Between musical drills, he worked on dance spins and perfected his autograph (dotting the "i" with a cute little heart) in preparation for his ascent. He roughed up some marketing ideas with Moon and decided to drop his last name.

With Moon's assistance, they prepared some demos of Prince's music. Moon weighed in on the lyrics, pitching Prince on a little idea he had, called "implied naughty sexuality." He figured some highly suggestive, but not too explicit language would get them past radio censors and generate big-time sales off the wink-wink, nudge-nudge buzz. It just might be the angle to launch the eager teen's career.

One of the first outcomes of this lyrical approach was the naughty innuendo of "SOFT AND WET." Taking complete solo command for the first time, the self-reliant kid used Moon's lyrical framework to build an entire song on his own—writing the music, recording each individual instrument and vocal line, then arranging the whole amazing thing together…all by himself.

Pleased with the result, Prince struck out to New York in search of a record deal. When he immediately began running into walls, Moon referred him to a local Minneapolis ad guy and concert promoter who had some Hollywood connections. The professional marketer honed his presentation and secured some meetings with the majors.

The strength of the demo and a great spin about the "next Stevie Wonder" touched off a bidding war, and in 1977 Warner Bros. signed him to an historic deal. Under the advocacy of Warner Bros. Chairman Mo Ostin, Prince was granted three albums instead of the standard single-LP contract and, following a studio test secretly observed by the management team, he was also awarded the uncommon clause of being able to produce his own work.

So it was that an unknown multi-instrumentalist with a one-word name became the youngest producer in the label's history. The fact that he was black made it all the more astounding. From the first moment of his career, Prince was a unique event.

In the hands of his new management and a new record company, Prince set up shop at a California studio and went about the work of crafting a debut album. Driven to do it all himself, he spent exhaustive time in the studio—12 to 14 hours a day—recording and re-recording every instrumental and vocal track. He rabidly embraced the new synthesizer technologies that were available to him and used them to invent a new sound that would be uniquely identifiable as his own. He multi-tracked the synths into full ensemble sounds and used them to create rhythmic accents almost like horns. As it turned out, the keyboard textures he instituted on this first record set the tune for much of pop music in the '80s, a style that became known as "the Minneapolis Sound."

Prince's debut album, entitled *For You*, was released a year later—into a world of *Saturday Night Fever* and *Grease* lightning. The lead single was Chris Moon's lyrical brainchild, "Soft and Wet," and it hit the radio waves on June 7, 1978—Prince's 20th birthday. True to its design, the suggestive title caught the wary but titillated eye of deejays and helped to advance the single to #12 on the Soul chart.

Beyond that fleeting notice, however, Prince's first album didn't see much success. Nonetheless, critics and industry watchers remained upbeat. Although much of the songcraft was uninspiring, it showcased the prodigy's amazing capabilities. By multi-tracking his own vocals on the album's intro, he created an almost classical chorale. At the record's close, he tore up some heavy electric guitar. In between, he shuffled across a bridge of pop, soul, rock and disco.

After all was said and done, he was still one of the most exciting events in modern pop history: a 20-year-old prodigy with a one-word name (his real name!) who wrote all his own music and sang, played and produced every note himself on his first LP. It was an uncommon achievement in the late 1970s.

The album and its lead single made several imprints that would ripple throughout his career. It introduced Prince's falsetto—a disco-era holdover and a more comfortable range for the post-adolescent teen—and it gave birth to his ethereally sexual identity. The juicy imagery of his debut single was reinforced by a provocative dust cover: Prince sitting nude on a space-traveling bed with a guitar carefully concealing his lap.

One of the most resounding impacts of this debut work was the way it established complete control as Prince's operating standard. The credits boldly spelled out every accomplishment on his résumé—"produced, arranged, composed and performed by Prince"—and the dust cover listed out each of the 27 instruments he'd used in the mix. In another mark of the young loner's fierce independence, Prince showed a militant aversion to being categorized, and from this very first record, he sought to span far-reaching genres. "Soft and Wet" was as much pop as it was R&B, and coming from a would-be megastar, it aimed for the widest possible appeal.

For the stargazing Minneapolitan, the sales of this first album were less than fulfilling, reaching only 150,000 units that year. Equally disappointing was the fact that, in spite of all his work to squirm past an R&B label, nearly all of the record's buyers were black. He'd been swooped up by the teenybopper soul magazines (*Right On!* and *Black Beat*) and cast as a pin-up boy instead of the highly original artist he intended to be.

TRACK 3: "I WANNA BE YOUR LOVER"

Following the weak launch of his career, Prince replaced his management team—dropping the hometown amateur who'd started him out and hiring a professional Hollywood firm—then returned to the studio to restart his star-making machine. He needed a hit this time. Bringing 20 new songs to the recording sessions, he laid the best nine into a new album, working much more rapidly this time around. As if to ignore his first release, the new album was titled merely *Prince*, a self-titled introduction more fitting for a debut.

Holding fast to his original vision, Prince applied the exact same recipe he used on *For You*, but this time, he turned up the heat on all the burners. Stylistically, the material was even more deliberate in its attempt to cross categories—from the formative funk of "Sexy Dancer" to the Van Halen-ish "Bambi" to a tune called "Still Waiting" that almost strayed toward country. His patented synth textures were thicker than ever, and once again, it was all a one-prodigy show (entirely "produced, arranged, composed and performed by Prince").

He spiked the tunes with an increased measure of licentious lyrics. (On one cut, Prince tries to convert a lesbian.) And once again, there was more nude cover art. This time, the back cover showed the bare-assed loverboy riding a winged horse. On the front cover, he posed demurely, fawning with his doe-like eyes and bearing his naked chest. Cropped neatly across the nipples, the photo offered the intriguing possibility that a full-length version would reveal more of Prince than the little girls could handle.

If his first album hadn't won over the world, it *had* made Prince a respected celebrity figure at home, and that confidence gave the new record a jolt. Cut more loosely, the tunes had more vitality, and the heightened sexual content gave the testosterone-laden lad more fruitful territory to romp around. There was a lustful edge that couldn't be ignored.

Under the gun to produce a hit, the little achiever delivered big. Several of the tracks had strong hooks. One of them, "I Feel for You," would become an enduring smash when Chaka Khan remade it five years later. As for himself, he pinned his hopes for commercial breakthrough to "I WANNA BE YOUR LOVER," an eager pony that harnessed disco, pop and R&B. Applying some "implied naughty sexuality," the hopeful lover tells his prospective girlfriend that he wants to be the only one she comes for.

This time, the plan worked. In the summer of 1979, "I Wanna Be Your Lover" reached #1 on the Soul chart and knocked on the door of the Pop Top 10. By the time it was all over, his concoction of musical crossbreeding and suggestive nastiness would sell more than a million copies. He'd done it; and he'd proved to himself, Warner Bros. and the world that this young Napoleon couldn't be denied.

TRACK 4: "HEAD"

In the early 1980s, small crowds of black fans gathered to catch the new sensation on his first concert circuits. He started out playing as a headliner in clubs and later graduated up to larger venues as the opening act for Rick James. Concertgoers showed up expecting to see the wannabe lover who, on radio, sounded like Michael Jackson with bigger testicles. What they got was something altogether different.

On stage, Prince's musical vision took on a startling, exaggerated form. Shocked audiences watched as the tiny bottle rocket militantly defied every R&B stereotype and humped the crowd's leg with flaming inhibition. His implied naughty sexuality became just plain naughty.

Prince the stage performer introduced a saucy new style that made the girls' blood pressure rise and had the guys rethinking their bedroom technique. He was a sweaty hyena, panting with sex. At his most heated moments, he stripped down to only bikini underwear—zebra-striped ones at that. (Boy George once described him as "a midget dipped in oil and rolled in pubic hair," and the women seemed to love every moist strand.)

Dancing like a whirling dervish, he embraced all the possibilities of the microphone's phallic form. Taking his sexcapades over the top, he introduced a new tune to the set called "HEAD" that was more devilishly crude than implicitly naughty. In case there was any doubt of its meaning, a female band member simulated a blow job on Prince while the little pervert spouted some stained pillow talk.

The song's funk groove pumped with sexual drive; its lyrics oozed with kinky sleaze. But what was most shocking was the intimate way in which he shared his fantasy. The fragileness of his falsetto whisper made his ruminations on being sucked off uncomfortably personal. It intimated the vulnerability of nakedness, the privacy of secret thoughts. It was downright embarrassing to listen to—like you'd caught somebody masturbating. He lured you in with his irresistible funk, and then made you feel the shame and thrill of an unwitting voyeur.

Prince's unrestrained stage antics were mesmerizing, and it gave a hard thrust to his showmanship. His stage presence was astounding. He dropped from spins to splits with more energy than James Brown and strut his stuff with Mick Jagger's cocksure swagger. He had more libido than a teen about to get laid. He was a delirious dynamo, dancing at center stage like a demon possessed, then slithering to a corner to masturbate the shaft of his lubricated guitar. (As his onstage routine grew more elaborate, the guitar was rigged up to spurt the crowd with a liquid ejaculation.)

Throbbing with sexual energy, Prince's show was electric. It was almost impossible to imagine how such a quiet, withdrawn kid could command such breathtaking stage charisma. But this was more than just a performance for Prince. It was an awakening to the world. And he'd woken up with a hard-on.

A withdrawn kid found a way to connect, and Prince created a visceral bond with concertgoers like few before him. There was an unusual energy inside a Prince show. It was as if a yearning spirit wanted to clutch your soul.

All the controversy surrounding the precocious newcomer attracted growing numbers of thrill-seekers to his concerts, and by the end of his second tour, people lined up for hours to covet a ticket for his notoriously provocative show. The breakthrough nature of his act also ensured that the critics would be watching, and his scintillating stage routine generated a flash through the news circuits: be on the lookout for the most exciting musical phenomenon in years.

Track 5: "Dirty Mind"

In the basement of his first house, the recluse had set up a 16-track recorder where he was throwing together tunes at an increasingly rapid pace. The adrenaline rush of watching his dream unfold hastened his already prolific production rate. On top of that, his sexual awakening gave him virtually unlimited material. He had all kinds of metaphors and wet dreams to relate, and he often recorded through the night in his wired cellar, finishing entire fantasies by morning.

With his saucy material in hand, Prince formed a new plan for achieving crossover. Rather than getting there by traveling middle-of-the-road, he would get there by going underground. He would reinvent himself as an alternative act and, in the process, break himself free of his R&B chains.

From the course collection of basement smut, Prince put together the pieces for a new album, leaving the production deliberately raw to give the tracks a distinctively punk vibe. The final product was a radical act, a glimpse under a flasher's trench coat that would stun the world and set him apart.

Prince's lead manager, an L.A. pro named Steve Fargnoli, was a willful cohort in Prince's subversive strategy. He believed in the breakthrough nature of the work, and he lobbied hard to get the new "basement tapes" released.

Warner Bros. was hesitant about the controversial content of the new songs. The lyrics guaranteed a complete lockout from radio airplay. Fargnoli argued, however, that the shock factor was just the thing to get their nitro-filled talent positioned for greatness. It would build a hardcore fan base among the alternative white-rock populace and garner the much-needed support of critics. It would generate excitement and elevate him as an icon. It would set the star up for a commercial breakthrough like one the company had never seen.

Fargnoli's persistence eventually won out, and in 1980, Prince released *Dirty Mind*, a torrid statement of rebellion that forever changed his career. The album cover showed the little outrage from stage in all his freakish perversity. It was a grainy, black-and-white photo—a glimpse into a shadowy underworld—and in front of a backdrop of old metal bedsprings, Prince posed in defiance, wearing the uniform of a punk warrior in heat. An open, rhinestoned suit coat revealed little except the skimpiness of his black bikini briefs.

On the back cover, the song titles were hastily spray-painted onto a wall by a militant delinquent.

Opening with the title track—"DIRTY MIND"—the new album unleashed Prince's assertive sexuality, and it did so with a pumping insistence that couldn't be denied. With a driving drumbeat that was more New Wave than R&B, the lead track confounded expectations. The minimalist instrumentation harkened more toward the Talking Heads and B-52s than any black-skinned artist of the day. This was definitely *not* the next Stevie Wonder.

It was the outrageous lyrical content that caused the biggest stir. Some of the content on the album was so depraved it was sinister. In addition to the homage to "Head," his dirty mind contemplated other shockers like "Sister," an urgent rocker about incest. It was all way too fiery for retailers and deejays to handle, and the album became an illicit thrill that was kept mostly under the mattress. As Michael Jackson's *Off the Wall* filled parents' living rooms with puppy love that year, *Dirty Mind* was doing naughty things in the bedroom.

For Prince, time alone in the basement studio was an opportunity for orgasmic self-gratification, and *Dirty Mind* provided a clear view through the keyhole of all that naughty fun. Like any private stroke, it was devoid of emotion, but it enjoyed all manner of taboo dreams.

True to the projections of Prince's collaborating management, the *Dirty Mind* project changed everything. It proclaimed the prodigy's disregard for convention. It shaped his flashpoint image and established him as a cult icon. Overnight, it transformed him from a pretty face behind a hit single to an "album artist" weaving a world-altering career like Lennon or Dylan. It put him on the edge. And at a time when black R&B and white rock n' roll were sharply divided along color lines, it broke him free of the disco-soul prison.

As expected, the critics were beside themselves. The *New York Times* called him "heir to the defiant rock n' roll tradition of Elvis Presley, Mick Jagger and Jimi Hendrix." The *Village Voice* proclaimed, "Rock in the eighties has a new Prince." The *Detroit News* christened him "the best soul-rock crossover talent of his age, a refreshing innovator in a time of stagnation." Even the rock bible *Rolling Stone* was abuzz with excitement, rating *Dirty Mind* with four-and-a-half out of five stars.

It was official: Prince was an original.

TRACK 6: "UPTOWN"

With his work on *Dirty Mind*, Prince forged deeply into white-rock territory. While his first two albums were written mostly on piano, the bulk of *Dirty Mind* was written on his Fender Telecaster guitar, and the result was a crossover sound more tailored to the alternative white scene. (His "When You Were Mine" was a quintessential rock riff.) It was a deliberate effort to draw more diversity into his tent, to create a unique musical community—a utopia he called "UPTOWN." In a song about the place, Prince united a legion of multi-ethnic partiers, a mix of races whose different skin colors were obscured by the lights on the dance floor. In "Uptown," individuality was something to be respected, worshipped and celebrated. Labels were strictly forbidden, and at one point in the lyrical tale, Prince defiantly shot down a girl's attempt to peg him as "gay."

Mixing white and black textures, a prancing synth line and a butch beat, Prince aggressively advanced his agenda of artistic androgyny. "Uptown" was a socio-political manifesto from a 21-year-old insurgent. Prince was a child of the '60s, and the neo-hippie created his own Haight-Ashbury: ideological convergence on the dance floor.

On stage, Prince's band lineup was also configured for crossover, and his shows looked and sounded more like alternative punk rock than anything that resembled R&B. Borrowing a page from his idol Sly Stone, his performance troupe was a surprising conglomeration of characters that personified his musical melting pot. It was an uncommon union of girls and boys, blacks and whites, funk players and jazz artists. His old friend André was there on bass and was accompanied up front by a black guitar player (Dez Dickerson). In the back, he put one white guy on drums and another (Matt a.k.a. "Doctor" Fink) on keyboards. On a second set of keyboards, he staffed a white woman—Lisa Coleman, a classically trained pianist.

The band's look was outlandish and carried a heavy New Wave-punk bravado. Dez colorfully dyed his hair and appointed himself with safety pins. Doctor Fink, complete with O.R. scrubs and a surgical mask, jerked behind his keyboards like an immigrant from Devo. Prince had even deflated his black-pride Afro and now wore long, grimy locks.

Musically, the band represented a startling collision of forces. The two-keyboard setup made for a super-charged synth sound akin to the New Wave pop of the Cars, the Police and Gary Numan. But standing up front were two rock guitarists who stood shoulder to shoulder dueling their metal wire. The lead singer—a black kid!—sang in an R&B falsetto.

When out doing promotional duty, Prince fully adopted the punk-rocker act. He wore a flasher's trench coat and a pin that said "Rude Boy." During his first major television appearance, performing on *American Bandstand* in early 1980 to promote "I Wanna Be Your Lover," he got sassy with Dick Clark. When the industry godfather queried Prince about his budding stardom, the smug freako refused to give any verbal responses. He merely shook his head and then held up some fingers when asked about the length of his career. During a high-energy performance on *Saturday Night Live*, he kicked over the microphone stand in classic punk rage.

On his tours through the news media circuit, the soft-spoken introvert dealt with his discomfort in an antagonistic way. Acting somewhat bratty with his interrogators, he played loose with the truth. He masterfully used hyperbole, obfuscation and, sometimes, silent refusal as devices to build his myth.

In his continuing quest to dodge categorization and court the white crowd, he even resorted to lying about his parentage, capitalizing on his light-brown skin to color his ethnicity as more mixed than it actually was. It started out with some elusive tidbits about his "complex" genealogy, and somewhere along the line, *Rolling Stone* got the notion that his father was half-black and his mother was

Italian. In fact, both parents were black; but pretty soon, Prince was telling the white lie too.

The smudging of lines didn't end with race. On stage, the shirtless Prince slipped on high-heeled shoes and legwarmers that questioned his sexuality. He didn't seem completely straight; he wasn't quite gay. He was aggressively ambiguous. Breaking every remaining taboo, the pansexual polymath sang in a girlish falsetto while manhandling his macho Stratocaster, then crossed the color line to french-kiss the white woman playing on keys.

By now it was apparent that the little incendiary had a grand purpose that transcended simple songcraft. This was a package to present himself as the reconciliation of a nation's dichotomies. A light-skinned black from America's Great White Heartland, he would be the nexus of a bi-racial society—the intersection of rock and soul.

TRACK 7: "COOL"

Prince wasn't the only artist making noise in 1981. On the black side of the radio dial, there was a swaggering new group called the Time. The all-male band had booties shakin' with a badass funk single entitled "COOL." Inspired by a self-assured bass line and an in-your-face attitude to match, the song strutted confidently into the Soul Top 10.

On their self-titled album cover, the six-member group had the air of a pimp mafia. Prowling the streets in zoot suits and fedora hats, they looked like they'd kill someone for scuffing their spit-polished shoes. The frontman was Morris Day, a bandmate from Prince's teenage neighborhood. The backing crew was formed from another local Minneapolis band, Flyte Tyme, and included powerhouse producers-in-waiting "Jimmy Jam" Harris and Terry Lewis.

Constructed around Morris Day's over-the-top braggadocio, "Cool" was the group's calling card, and the lead hitman performed a hilarious caricature of a superstar ego. Morris boasted about his fancy cars and his "Stellas." On stage, he primped in a mirror and beckoned his personal valet to come straighten his suit. It was comically colossal cool.

The Time was an instant hit with black audiences. Their dance-oriented funk n' roll sound was infectious, and Morris' uproarious gigolo act was fantastically charismatic. In his patented nasal pimp-sneer, Morris told audiences, "Ain't nobody bad like me!" After a few minutes of Morris' self-promotion and the band's cocky groove, many were convinced that this *was* the ultimate funk band.

Many industry observers focused in on the name Jamie Starr listed as a lead producer of the Time's debut. They were curious to uncover the genius behind R&B's hottest up-and-comers. A Twin Cities reporter, Jon Bream, was among the first to hunt Starr down, and he emerged with a fantastic notion. Bream contended that Jamie Starr did not exist, that the moniker was actually a guise for Prince, and that Minneapolis' prodigy was the real wizard at work, controlling all the knobs behind a heavy curtain.

It seemed impossible, but it was true. The 23-year-old punk-crossover sensation was surreptitiously making his move on the black scene. Both Morris and Prince denied his involvement, but over time the veil of their lies wore thin.

As it turned out, Prince had concocted the whole project as a new creative outlet for himself. In meetings with Warner Bros., he cut a deal to create a ventriloquist act with which to vent a whole other side of his musical personality. In his basement studio, Prince single-handedly developed the material for the group's debut LP—the lyrics, the rhythm tracks, the guitar solos, everything. He then brought Morris into his studio, re-recorded the lead voice track with Morris up front and swapped out his own guide vocals. The band's album was complete before the rest of the band was even formed.

In retrospect, it's almost silly to listen to. When Morris intros the back-up girls, Prince's falsetto chimes in. When Morris calls the band, several Princes reply. Prince even steals one of the lead lines for himself.

With this stealth R&B takeover, the ambition and ability of the mysterious imp appeared more awesome than ever. As an artist, his reach extended twice as far. As a would-be monarch, he had the beginnings of an empire.

TRACK 8: "SEXUALITY"

What was buried beneath all the jizz and saliva covering his records was the fact that Prince was a deeply religious guy. During his tormented youth, the Seventh-Day Adventist Church had been an important pillar, and the faith's urgent warnings about Christ's Second Coming were emblazoned upon his soul. These religious sensibilities didn't mesh too well with songs about incest and blowjobs. His own father had expressed strong disapproval, as did hundreds of other morality watchdogs. One of his original band members and closest confidantes had bolted when his shock tactics got too sleazy for her Jesus-loving soul.

Faced by an obvious conflict with traditional religious precepts, the prodigal genius authored his own. His follow-up to *Dirty Mind*—the kid's fourth album—was entitled *Controversy*, and it was the opening event in a decade-long campaign to reconcile the sacred with his naughty sexuality. Newspaper headlines printed on the album cover pointed to Prince's Christian ideals: "Love Thy Neighbor," "Free Food Stamps for Good Samaritans," "Annie Christian [read "anti-Christ"] Sentenced to Die." But the track listing—including "Jack U Off" and "Do Me, Baby"—suggested plenty more luridness inside. A promo photo caught the rude boy posing in black briefs in a shower, but a crucifix hanging beside him in the stall gave a different character to the cleansing.

In his first presentation as a serious "message" artist, Prince delivered his new manifesto in a song called "SEXUALITY." Disgusted by the way social intolerance made a controversy of race, sexual orientation and religious views, he offered naked inhibition as the cure. According to Prince's unique theology, there'd be peace and harmony in the world if we'd all see each other as the Lord does—by stripping off our constricting underwear. In an urgent rallying speech, Prince championed a doctrine: spiritual salvation through physical liberation. On "Do Me, Baby," he promised to keep humping until the Judgment Day and ended the song with an extended verbalization of his own orgasm. On the title track, he recited the Lord's Prayer while a throbbing beat made love to the dance floor.

Along with his new doctrine came a growing sense of self-importance. Several people in his camp viewed his talents as nothing less than the work of God. The media hailed him as rock's messiah. His personal story contained all the drama of Phoenix-like ascendance. And now, Prince had a holy purpose. Suddenly, his career was more than a teenager's dream. It was a divine calling.

The tour that supported *Controversy* made high theater of Prince's newly christened ministry. As the show started, the stage was bathed in billowing fog and ghostly purple light. A tape played an a cappella gospel intro that warned of the impending Second Coming of the Lord. A spotlight suddenly revealed Prince's silhouette on a high catwalk, and in a seemingly heretical twist to his God-fearing opener, Prince dove into his nasty vaudeville of sexual liberty. His stage gymnastics featured a risqué striptease, lots more "Head" and another masturbation act with his guitar.

The bank of fog returned for the closer, "Sexuality," and during the final strains, a white cross illuminated on the backdrop as Prince made his way up onto the catwalk again. Silhouetted in front of the cross, he posed with his arms outstretched, creating the illusion of his own crucifixion.

Weighted by the tension of his new religious politics, *Controversy* was a lot less fun, and the critics were more muted in their praise. Nonetheless, Prince continued to forge new ground. In an electric surge of hyper creation, his production techniques made a jump to light speed, and like an unchained stallion, he shrieked, he bucked, and he thrashed. Literally, he dropped aural bombs. At times, he got so fired up by his seminal abilities that he burst into the piercing screams that became his trademark.

Similar to his last LP, most of the material was aimed directly at the feet. If Prince was gathering his followers, he was building his church on the dance floor. And he was recruiting a congregation of both blacks and whites. Musically, he continued his quest to find a hybrid sound, and he used arcs of electronics to straddle white and black genres. It was New Wave funk and R&B punk.

In the quest for crossover, Prince made several adjustments to sharpen his presentation to a broader audience. Though he kept the trench coat and Cuban high heels, he replaced the bikini shorts and thigh highs with a tuxedo shirt and slacks. He also performed many of the new songs (including "Sexuality") in his more "manly" lower register, dropping the "R&B" falsetto in favor of a more "rock and roll" voice.

Meanwhile, Steve Fargnoli worked to broaden Prince's access within rock circles. He landed him a warm-up slot on the Rolling Stone's 1981 stadium tour. It was a golden opportunity to whiten his exposure.

On October 9, 1981, the little-known black rocker joined the bill for the Stone's L.A. opener, taking his place on a long queue of warm-up acts that included the J. Geils Band and George Thorogood. In a surreal contrast of scale, the tiny Minneapolitan stood before a crowd of almost 50,000 pale faces. Mustering every ounce of confidence, he charged boldly into his alternative funk-rock.

Within minutes, however, the crowd turned ugly. Impatient viewers in the front rows began heckling the prissy black punk with abuse. Pretty soon, trash was being lobbed onto the stage. Prince heroically held his ground for 20 minutes and then stormed off the stage in disgrace.

It was clear that Prince still had a long way to go before winning white America. Only one thing could get him the acceptance he craved: he needed a big hit on mainstream radio.

TRACK 9: "NASTY GIRL"

Prince continued his crusade unabated. Hunkering down in his basement studio, he cloistered himself in his music with Calvinist dedication. In his sleepless recording frenzies, the workaholic often outlasted three shifts of engineers. He started appearing less in public and stopped talking to the press.

The media silence made his mystery to the public all the more magnetic.

At the same time, he built a structure around him that would support his sacred mission. He hired a bodyguard and personal servant, a huge man named "Big Chick" Huntsberry. At 6'6" and 320 lbs. and with balding, long white hair and lots of tattoos, Big Chick looked like he'd stepped out of a WWF championship ring. Beside his diminutive boss, the ludicrously large handler appeared all the more gargantuan. He became a wall of protection, a barrier that would preserve Prince's God-given artistry from wasteful disruptions and protect His Royal Shyness from the public's growing scrutiny. With Big Chick managing the mundane aspects of everyday life, Prince locked himself in the studio for 15-24 hours on end.

In the studio, he had discovered a new toy: the Linn drum machine, a state-of-the-art technology for electronic rhythm making. The fresh invention gave him fresh inspiration, and it resulted in a new, more innovative dance sound. He used this inventory of new material to expand the cottage industry he began with the Time. For his next incarnation, he created a girl group.

Denise Matthews was a gorgeous bracelet that Rick James wore around at the time. She had the same trans-racial look as Prince: light-brown skin, wavy, dark hair, and thin nose and mouth lines. She was the perfect line extension for his integrative vision. Plus, Denise had something more. An amateur actress in soft-porn flicks, she knew her way around the bedroom, and she'd have no problem giving up a little skin for public consumption. What better First Lady for the Sultan of Sex? Prince saw great possibilities in her figure and lured her away from James with a record deal.

Prince had the whole concept figured out beforehand. The group's leader would be named Vagina, her backing group would be the Hookers, and the ensuing controversy would shoot the new act straight to the top. Leveler minds prevailed, however, and Denise went public with a more innocuous name: Vanity. Prince added two girls from his camp as sidekicks (one white and one black, of course), and he dubbed the trio Vanity 6, allegedly in reference to their "titty count."

On the group's self-titled LP, Prince once again challenged the limits of sexual jurisprudence. The album's cover art showed the three women in lingerie, and the song titles included "Wet Dream." The whole package had the stilted pose and airbrushed haze of a *Penthouse* spread. "Nasty Girl" was the leadoff single and the headline for their leather-and-lace expose. To a striptease rhythm that found a welcome home in topless joints, Vanity crooned that she required at least seven inches from her man. It was full-blown Sexuality put into practice.

Like all *Penthouse* centerfolds, you couldn't take their fantasy fuck too seriously. Their act was only skin-deep, and their limp vocals showed it. Unintentionally perhaps, they served themselves up as an enjoyable, camp novelty.

The strength of the concept—a pre-Madonna Madonna who asserted her girl power through sex—was undermined by the awkward reality that Vanity was merely a puppet for Prince. As expected, though, the blue act caught some attention, and the whiz-kid boss scored another strong hit. Opening a red-light district in the record shop, the LP drew half a million eager customers and reached #6 on the Black chart.

For Prince, "Nasty Girl" was the flagship for a new ultra-synthetic dance sound. Mastering the technologies of the budding computer age, the studio wizard used electronics throughout: drum machines, synth bass and microprocessor modulations aplenty. He created an implosive "dead drum" sound that—coupled with his synth-generated charms—became a hypnotic force on the dance floor for years to come.

TRACK 10: "IF A GIRL ANSWERS (DON'T HANG UP)"

The output of Prince's recent recording binge included a second album for the Time, entitled *What Time is It?*. The LP was loaded with hit material, and it secured the group's enduring popularity. Three of the album's six songs scored well on the Black chart (including the #1 hit "777-9311"), and their success delivered a high-voltage charge to Prince's swelling career.

As with his first Time project, this latest material was almost entirely Prince. From opening drumbeat to closing synth chord, Prince was the singular artistic force driving all aspects of the Time's new LP. This time around, however, Prince played his puppetry as more of a joke. On both *What Time Is It?* and *Vanity 6*, he played cat and mouse with a series of crediting deceptions, peppering the liner notes with bogus songwriting notations.

(Another secret hit around this time was the 1983 Stevie Nicks single "Stand Back." Although he was concealed in the credits, he dropped the synth riff that sent a decent song to the top of the charts.)

On his side projects, Prince also sneaked in some humorous cameos, disguising himself with unexpected character roles. One of the most surprising moments appeared on Vanity's disc. "IF A GIRL ANSWERS (DON'T HANG UP)" captures a hilarious battle of trash-talking when Vanity places a call to her boyfriend and finds a rival lover on the other end of the phone. The scene quickly becomes an all-out brawl of wits, a volley of insults that highlights Prince's biting sense of humor. The real joke in the interplay, however, is that the other girlfriend isn't actually a woman. It's Prince, doing the part of a nasally bitch.

With time, the extent of Prince's involvement in both Vanity 6 and the Time proved to be even greater than expected. Not only were the notes all his, he also directed the outfits, the dance steps, the hairdos, and even the way his protégés walked and talked. The marionette controlled every movement.

The vision that seized the punk Napoleon was so self-perceived that it left little room for outside perspectives. Preparing for the Time's first public appearances, he ran the group through long hours of performance drills, staging the choreography and arranging their instrumentals. The general let no detail fall outside his grasp, and he demanded every ounce of excellence that his subjects could muster.

At times, his firm grip got painful. On the road, the Time served as Prince's warm-up act, but when their hilariously entertaining show threatened to eclipse the boss' own messianic spectacle, the little demagogue sometimes booted them from the billing. Strings of tension began to wind tighter.

It didn't take long for Prince's totalitarianism to generate an uprising. Two of the most significant talents—Jimmy "Jam" Harris and Terry Lewis—were the first to leave. Their creativity was too large to be oppressed by Prince's autocratic controls. Behind the master's back, they began producing outside acts, and when it conflicted with their Time, they were summarily fired from the band.

For Prince, the departure of Jimmy Jam and Terry Lewis turned out to be an unexpected boon to his empire and his legend. The pair of protégés quickly became one of the leading production teams in pop and R&B history, with more than a dozen #1 hits. Their work over the years involved monster smashes for some of the most recognizable artists of the '80s and '90s, including Janet Jackson (they orchestrated Ms. Jackson's big break with *Control* in 1985), Boyz II Men, New Edition and Mary J. Blige. In the process, they pollinated late 20th-century pop with strains of Princely sound.

For those who remained in Prince's feudal kingdom, the relationship with their lordship grew more distant every day. Planting himself more firmly on his throne, Prince remained largely removed from his underlings, appearing among them only to direct his vision or shake the stick at a rehearsal. Almost all of his planning and confiding was done in private conference with Steve Fargnoli, and after his brief sorties into public, he immediately returned to the sanctuary of Big Chick's blockade. Newcomers to the troupe received strict instructions: don't speak to him unless spoken to.

The detachment took its toll, and by early 1982 his teenage buddy and musical soulmate André left the fold. He'd been driven out by the growing gloom of his best friend's shadow. In the ensuing years, André's career rarely saw the sun. After a few failed solo albums, he steered his way to production (including work with one-time wife Jody Watley), while Prince alone scaled the heights of their basement dreams.

TRACK 11: "1999"

By 1982 Prince had stirred up a lot of excitement in the music industry. He'd caught the critic's collective eye, and music writers everywhere were on the edge of their seats in anticipation of his next arrival. What was delivered that year astounded even the most prophetic of rock's sages.

On October 27, just 12 months since his last issue, the commercially nubile artist released a *double* album. It was unthinkably monstrous: four sides of new material, all of it "produced, arranged, composed and performed" by the multi-instrumental wunderkind—the same wunderkind who was redefining stage performance and was the reputed marionette behind two of R&B's most eventful side acts.

The album had a very big title: *1999*. The millennial date suggested a vision so huge that it promised life-changing revelations.

The two-record set was packaged in purple, the color of sexuality, royalty and divinity. The cover art, a hand drawing by the prodigy himself, featured lots of little images from his meta-sexual ministry: a stairway to enlightenment, a phallic "1," a pubic-haired "P" and a meld of the male and female sex symbols—the inception of his famous, unpronounceable naming device. The mysterious, photo-less cover art also instituted a new language convention: an alphanumeric shorthand that became more involved over time (eventually replacing the first-person pronoun with a pictogram of an eye) and later became a standard for the hip-hop nation and instant-message writers everywhere.

Another significant marking on the purple package was a tiny, backwards reference to his band, which he dubbed "the Revolution." The group's name proved again that Prince viewed his work as nothing less than a cultural *jihad*.

The title track—"1999"—was his siren call for sexual-spiritual revelation, and it gave his doctrine of Sexuality some apocalyptic urgency. The turn of the millennium was Prince's metaphor for the end of the world. On that day, the world would turn purple as red blood rained down against a blue sky. It was a vision of nuclear holocaust, the Armageddon that would return us all to our Maker. And its imminence meant we had to get enlightened fast—by embracing Sexuality.

It was classic 'carpe diem,' but with a hedonistic twist. Prince's celebration would be a party of the flesh, and in anticipation of the Second Coming, he called on his celebrants to rejoice with sex and dancing. The song "1999" was a holy communion of genres, and once again, he built his church squarely on the dance floor. Over a propulsive beat and synth anthem, big cymbal crashes punctuated the mix like nuclear flashes to mark the end of time. At the opener, different band members took a turn at the mic to deliver the messianic message.

The next five tracks on the record were an amalgam—either in principle or in practice—of his notions of sexual liberation and transcendental fucking. Prince wanted to let your hair down, undress you and show you a better place to die. Indeed, *1999* was a party to die for, and Prince threw an epoch bash.

The *1999* project marked the official arrival of Prince the computer wizard. Like his Vanity product, his new material was heavily chip-driven. Playing out his "Nasty Girl" mechanics to completion, he advanced a new standard for '80s pop with his synthetic dance sounds. The Linn drum machine supplied untiring rhythms, and it was obvious the sleepless studio technician had met his soulmate. Unstoppably funky, inexhaustibly bountiful. Prince plugged in his ultimate sex toy and got off on its groove. He produced almost-techno rhythms that had an intoxicating effect and kept the action from leaving the dance floor. Only twice in 12 tracks did his perpetual-motion machine pause to take a breather. The ass-controlling power was inescapable. So enthralled was U.K. mag *Melody Maker* that its critic proclaimed *1999* "one of the most inspiring dance epics known to man."

1999 was a magnum opus of invention, the Young Funkenstein's crowning achievement. It was the grand masterpiece his talents had promised, the chef d'oeuvre of his genre-busting sound. High-tech yet raw, rocking yet funky, mysterious yet approachable, it wasn't black music, and it wasn't white. It was purple. It crossed categories, not because it straddled them, but rather, because it was its own format. For lack of a better description, the critics called it "techno funk," and in three record stores on one street, it would be filed in three different categories.

It was an artistic wonderment, and the world took notice. The two-disc set received almost-universal raves from critics. In a year full of accolades, it was the editors of *Rolling Stone* who handed Prince the highest of honor of them all: they named him 1982's "Artist of the Year."

TRACK 12: "LADY CAB DRIVER"

Prince's mass critical acceptance won him the cover of *Rolling Stone*, and the photo gave the general public its first close-up of rock's fiery comet. Decorated by Vanity on his side, the oversexed techno-funkateer carried all the eccentric bravado of a major star. He now wore his hair in a bouffant of curls à la Little Richard. A ruffled shirt and heavy eyeliner added to the glam androgyny. Yet somehow, he was still the sex-crazed punk that every mother feared. He wore a pimp's mustache—thin and stubbly—and a vinyl, studded trench coat. He stared luridly, with his lips parted slightly, anticipating the sweet taste of mama's little girl. He'd unbuttoned his shirt to reveal wiry curls of chest hair and placed his hand in his waistband as if reaching for more wiry curls below. It was a portrait of a sexual warrior, and it was an aggressive advance in his efforts to rewrite the nation's sexual code.

If there was anything unsettling about the *1999* project, it was the effectiveness with which he was creating his cult of Sexuality. The hypnotic beats of his album were an effective draw, and Prince lured millions of listeners into his self-contained sonic compound. With its electronic wiring and vast, tunnel-like construction, *1999* was a cold, subterranean bunker for the orgy that would end all time. But inside, things sometimes got a little scary.

Throbbing drum machines laid a relentless current for moaning guitar strains, shrieking vocals and discordant synths. It was a dark, hedonistic celebration, and all the lust and leering left little room for love. Critics noticed the void, and the *Los Angeles Times* wrote that *1999* showed "an undeniable emotional emptiness in the crucial center of the music." In fact, the two-disc set didn't contain a single love song.

Within his self-focused domain, Prince's lust often had threatening implications for women. His menacing beats harbored a sexual aggression that sometimes crossed the line to brutality. On "LADY CAB DRIVER," he purged a litany of social grievances by pumping his rap with coital thrusts—over female moans that often sounded more pained than participatory. At another unnerving point in the album, a panicked woman cried out from the sonic bunker, pleading for help.

In the dark coldness of his music, Prince revealed a deep-seeded lust for power and sexual domination—and a virtual vacuum of anything that resembled feelings of love.

TRACK 13: "LITTLE RED CORVETTE"

It all happened in the back seat of a little red car. Hushed breaths emanated from behind the steamy windows, and a piston turn—a whip snap—provided brief flashes of the kinky action inside. A raw, lusty whisper built to a hungry growl. Then, without warning, the car door was thrown open, and a killer pop chorus invited everyone to join in the backseat fun.

Released on February 9, 1983, "LITTLE RED CORVETTE" was the song that changed everything. It was Prince's first Top 10 Pop hit, and it drew throngs of new listeners to his music. The song was a wholly contrived piece of pop-rock bait. More decidedly rock n' roll than anything else on the album, it was the white knight that finally conquered mainstream radio.

As expected, Prince's radio breakthrough brought along with it the ears and minds of a whole generation of Middle American teens. It was another medium, however, that captured their souls. The real breakthrough vehicle for Prince was MTV. The fledgling channel was just beginning to hit its stride and was quickly proving its power for making and breaking careers. The videos that supported *1999* were the first videos by an African-American—along with Michael Jackson's *Thriller* films—to be anointed with the network's approval.

The video for "Little Red Corvette" was a straightforward song-and-dance routine—a stage performance lifted from his tour. No special effects. No storyline. Just a performer and his craft. And just as his shows had left critics and concertgoers mumbling, the video delivered a broad-scale punch. It was a smack-you-over-the-head display of stage charisma. The electric introduction of an entertainment wonder. Sublime talent. Pure magic.

The Prince on video was nothing close to the bikini-bearing freak of yore. His image had been toned way back for commercial breakthrough. Buttoned up in a full-length coat, he kept his more shocking exhibits under wraps. But from the way he moved, it was obvious something big wanted to bust its way out. The lust was palpable, but it simmered rather than boiled. Prince made his new audience anticipate his sex rather than experience the penetration. The seduction was powerful, and it offered a charged counterpoint to Michael Jackson's slick but asexual *Thriller*.

The booming success of "Little Red Corvette" was accompanied by other follow-up successes: the title track's ascension to #12, as well as his second Top 10 hit, "Delirious." Within the currents of pop culture, Prince's boat floated high. Crossover was complete. And *1999* became a multi-million-unit seller.

In late 1982, Prince put his social assault machinery on the road, launching a six-month U.S. concert sweep. He turned up the heat on his seduction of a nation, adding a flying bed to his extravaganza, but still keeping his pants on for maximum tease. He even cut the shows tantalizingly short—after little more than an hour—as if whetting the world's appetite for something really big to come. The critics were stumbling over themselves to find a better superlative.

As "Little Red Corvette" slowly took command of the airwaves, larger and larger crowds started mobbing the box office. Audiences eventually grew to 20,000, and the show rapidly became one of the biggest tours of 1983, grossing upwards of $10 million.

For the sprightly seducer, the victory was only partly about financials and acclaim. As his Little Red pill took effect, he watched his concert audiences grow whiter and whiter. By the last dates on the tour, there was a 50-50 integration of blacks and whites. He'd finally built his Uptown.

Playlist Two: Haughty Heights (1983-1986)

Track 1: "Purple Rain"

A movie had long been a part of the Plan. Prince loved the movies and seemed to have a healthy appreciation for the medium's power to subvert popular culture. A film would be the perfect vessel for bottling his image-rich vision. It would be his final, full-frontal assault.

Expectedly, the initial concept writing was an intensely private affair. During the *1999* tour, Prince often sat alone on the tour bus and in his dressing room—insular and detached behind Big Chick, his 320-pound curtain of flesh—busily downloading ideas into a purple notebook that was always at his side. The concept was a very personal one. It was a story about his life: his tumultuous upbringing and his struggle to succeed. The final script, brought to life by a professional screenwriter, told a story of moral failure and spiritual rebirth. And it carried all the apocalyptic urgency of his *1999* religion. Recalling his lyrical images of the Judgment Day (red blood in a blue sky), he named the film *Purple Rain*.

The plotline of the film would turn on his performance of the title anthem, "Purple Rain." In a sweeping rock ballad for the ages, Prince came to grips with his lustful, empty-hearted coldness and wept for forgiveness and salvation. With apologies, cleansing guitar chords and a soaring coda, he delivered his prayer for love: heartfelt wishes for victory over death, rapture in the Apocalypse. He only wanted to see his loved ones laughing in the purple rain.

Personally and professionally, *Purple Rain* would be a pinnacle achievement. But Prince's management was reluctant. The kid's fan base was still relatively modest, and no one on his management team had any real film experience. Steve Fargnoli pitched the idea to some major movie studios, but the proposal fell flat.

The star remained insistent, however, and the team set out to fund and produce the project independently. In their time of need, Prince's chief patriarch at Warner Bros., Chairman Mo Ostin, stepped in to support his artist's vision and pony up some cash to get them started.

Wrapping up the *1999* tour, Prince and company built camp at a suburban Minneapolis warehouse where they began preparations for a film shoot. Since the script was all about him, it could only be expected that his closest cohorts would play a major role. In fact, they played all the major roles. Members of his band, Vanity, Morris Day and the Time—all were to see serious action on screen. Even Big Chick would get his moment in the limelight. So the amateur troupe began intensive acting lessons and dance training. Prince ran his boot camp like a drill sergeant, showing obvious annoyance when anyone displayed less than absolute commitment.

It seemed highly unlikely that the product could ever succeed. Movies starring rock artists almost never succeeded. (A recent bomb by the more commercially proven Rick Springfield was only the latest example.) This film had a shoestring budget (only $7 million). The director had never filmed a project outside of college. None of the leads had ever acted before. The marquee star was hardly a household name, and his story was highly personal.

But several elements were converging to create an unstoppable force. Not the least of these were Prince's supernatural talent, passionate vision and unwavering drive. He practically *willed* the movie to greatness.

A critic from the *Los Angeles Herald Examiner* witnessed an early screening of a completed edit and emerged from beneath the shrouds with a fantastic pronouncement to the world. His headline read, "Prince Delivers the Best Rock Concert Film Ever Made."

Track 2: "Darling Nikki"

As his film was being pieced together in Los Angeles, Prince took up residence at Sunset Sound, a local recording studio where he worked to complete supporting music for the movie. The historic sessions were awash with inspired production. He was adrenalized with anticipation of the film, and the therapy of screenwriting his life seemed to bring a change of heart in his approach to music making.

In a new glasnost of spirit, Prince developed the work with his band and attributed it as a group project. All but three of the songs that found their way into the movie were the product of "Prince and the Revolution." Several of the tracks were recorded live—in his Minneapolis warehouse and during an historic gig at a local club called First Avenue—and then reworked in the studio.

Both of these devices—the live recordings and the presentation of a classic "working band" in the tradition of Bruce Springteen's E Street Band and Bob Seger's Silver Bullet Band—seemed to be deliberate attempts to borrow cues from the world of arena rock, and on the title track Prince climbed his own purple stairway to heaven.

The profile of the band took a dramatic turn with the addition of Wendy Melvoin, a guitarist who took the frontline slot left open by Dez Dickerson (another long-time servant who fled the feudal kingdom). A talented member of an accomplished musical family, Wendy was a childhood friend of keyboardist Lisa Coleman. With Wendy in the lineup, the group was now overwhelmingly white, and the pair of female pals quickly became a secondary axis of the band. The ultra-close girls added an intriguing twist to the package, and Prince readily channeled hints of their lesbianism.

In early 1984, Prince—with his Revolution—completed work on a nine-song soundtrack album, engineering it for final triumph. Strapping on his guitar like never before, he moved from "techno funk" to what critics called "dance rock"— a sound that was broadly appealing to white playlists. He even formatted the album for the charts. Sticking to a single disc this time, he cut the tunes shorter, making them friendlier to radio. It was economically concise and emotionally cohesive. And he played it safe by dropping the more sexual and overtly religious references.

The *Purple Rain* LP was an emotional concept album. The opening chord of a church organ and a sermon by the Minister left no doubt of its spiritual intent. Like *1999*, there was a raucous, fuck-the-Apocalypse party at the outset ("Let's Go Crazy"), but unlike *1999*, the rest of the album strived to love. A relationship bloomed on the second cut—"Take Me With You"—but went awry on "The Beautiful Ones" (they always hurt him). This magnificent ballad was his first recorded display of genuine emotion. Ghostly synths meandered like tormented souls through a chilly night, and at the song's climax, Prince unleashed his hurt in a wide-open scream. For several seconds, you could almost touch his bleeding soul.

As the album continued, the mood spiraled downward into the mechanical coldness of "Computer Blue," reaching an angry bottom at "DARLING NIKKI"— a raunchy paean to emotionless sex. The torrid, fuck-me grind—with its open reference to masturbation—immediately drew the ire of decency watchdogs. Ironically, the lyrics were pretty tame by earlier standards, but Prince's wickedly predatory music made them sound a whole lot worse. Tipper Gore led the charge against him, holding up his mention of masturbation as a family-values foul. She used the violation as impetus for building the Parents' Music Resource Center (PMRC), the organization that later won the fight to slap stickered warnings on records that contain adult content.

"Darling Nikki" ended with the sound of a rainstorm—*purple* rain, for sure— and it was here, at the record's lowest point of anger and lust, that Prince came to understand the error of his ways. In the coda, he placed a backward recording of human speech (a studio trick normally reserved for more satanic rockers). The reversed tape anticipated the return of his Lord. There was also a significant revelation in the liner notes. Immediately following the dirty lyrics of "Darling Nikki," the liner posted a note from "the Righteous 1" advising Prince to embrace love over lust.

The second side of *Purple Rain* opened with "When Doves Cry," an emotional turning point that opened a door to spiritual rebirth. Using richly Christian imagery, Prince then offered the ultimate expression of unconditional love: "I Would Die 4 U." With its high-octane rhythm, the song led a redemption sequence that ended the album with raptures of love: the emotional victory of a troubled, insular soul.

Track 3: "When Doves Cry"

The *Purple Rain* film followed the same redemption storyline as the record, and it added fictional flesh to Prince's journey of moral enlightenment. It was the tale of a kid from a broken family who had trouble with relationships. He was a controlling brat who shut people out of his life. He was unable to hold onto love, until he finally found peace with who he was, and he found that peace by discovering a bond with his father. The movie aggregated all the elements of his past that were legendary in his own mind: battles between hometown bands, his parents' destructive marriage, the refuge he found in his basement hideaway, his band members' nagging frustration with their despot.

Morris Day, with his diabolical, all-fun, no-depth ways, was cast as the villain. He was joined by his sidekick "valet," and together they provided some caustically comic relief. They vied against "the Kid" (as the purple protagonist was dubbed) and his pained struggle for enlightenment, in a battle to be top brass at the local club and the object of a girl's affection. Stricken by troubles at home, the Kid was a miserable runt, and he treated his women badly. He backhanded his bitch a few scenes after sending her topless into a frozen lake.

When Prince's problems reached their crushing peak—his fictional father attempted suicide—the Kid came close to following in his dad's tragic footsteps. In his moment of crisis, he suddenly discovered his father's music and the profound connection it implied. It was the turning point for a deeper understanding of love, one that brought a cleansing renewal of spirit and won him his final victory. Surprisingly, for a character as outlandish as Prince, the story had a gritty realism. It was grounded in the streets and played out in the dark alleys around nightclubs and the back halls of a crumbling home.

One of the last songs Prince created for the *Purple Rain* project was "WHEN DOVES CRY." It was a stunning song that captured all the heartache of his tangled introspection. Prince left the arrangement beautifully naked, yanking out the bass line to emphasize his signature synth and hypnotic drum machine. It started with an arresting fanfare of disoriented rock guitar and ended with classical keyboard runs that left the song hanging on a revelatory high. He stacked several vocal tracks together, bringing the many voices in his head into one harmonic melody. The coiled tension of the music placed the focus directly onto his deeply personal lyric, one that haunted you with its shadowy glimpses into a struggling soul.

Of at least five potential singles on the album, Prince picked "When Doves Cry" to launch his purple assault. The record company, however, was anxious about his selection. There was a lot of risk to leading off with such an unconventional song. And there was a lot riding on its success. But the Kid was in his zone. His instincts were dead-on. *1999* had made Prince a hot commodity, and radio markets were salivating for his edgy, innovative sound.

"When Doves Cry" was released on May 16, 1984, and it immediately sent shivers through the music world. The song shot to the top of the charts and was Warners' fastest-selling single yet. It went on to become the highest-grossing song of 1984.

TRACK 4: "EROTIC CITY"

Since *Purple Rain* involved both the Time and Vanity as integral characters, Prince took the occasion to create new music for both. In early 1984, he embarked on a third album for Morris Day and the increasingly fractured Time. The group continued to dissolve after Jam and Lewis's departure and was now jokingly referred to as Half Time.

The new Time album was an unoriginal pool-out, but it did contain a couple of commercial dance hits ("Jungle Love" and "The Bird") that were popularized by performances in the *Purple Rain* film. The biggest of them was "Jungle Love," which reached #6 on the Black chart and cracked the Pop Top 20.

That same year, Prince was also making progress on a second album for Vanity. His real-life lover and protégée was to play the female lead in the movie. But breakdown was occurring on that front as well. Following a combination of romantic and professional differences, Vanity left the camp.

The filming of her part in the movie was already set to begin, but a girl would-n't ruin it for Prince now. A mountain couldn't block his vision. Prince quickly ordered up a casting call, and a model from L.A. won the Vanity look-alike con-test. She was similarly trans-racial and adequately talented, and she passed an interview with the boss by professing her belief in God.

Prince dubbed her Apollonia, plucking the name from a character in *The Godfather*. Decorated in slutty make-up and scant lingerie, she obediently took her place as the stand-in for Vanity. The "musical" group Vanity 6 then became Apollonia 6. (The four backing titties remained the same).

At Sunset Sound, Prince quickly pulled together an LP for his new leading lady. Of course, he did this one totally solo. Both in look and sound, the self-titled disc was a complete rehash of the Vanity project two years before. It was another girlie poster in his workshop. He brought back the heavy synths and drum machines and conducted another "Nasty Girl"-type striptease. "Sex Shooter" was the lead single this time.

Although he painted all the strokes, the artist once again forgot to put his name on the canvas. But this time around, he was probably better off not receiv-ing the credit. The record was a rushed attempt at empire building, and it smacked of mass production. Like a hooker on the corner, it was worth a curious glance, but in spite of its shapely grooves, it was mostly a turn-off.

Prince's otherworldly product stream continued on the flipsides to his *Purple Rain* singles, where he dropped new tunes, like "17 Days," that were superior to most artists' album cuts. (Through the course of his career, Prince would release more than three dozen such B-side tracks, and although several—like "Horny Toad" and "Scarlet Pussy"—were kitschy, perverted novelties, many were top-rate tunes in their own right, like the oft-covered "How Come U Don't Call Me Anymore?" and "She's Always in My Hair.") In the Prince mania of 1984, one of the *Purple Rain* B-sides ignited a blaze in the dance-club underground. The back-side of "Let's Go Crazy" harbored an outlaw dance hit called "Erotic City." The pluck of a helium guitar string introduced a trudging three-note bass hook that buried itself in your groin. Against it, Prince layered a robotic synth line, an alien computer calculating the kink. Drum machines lashed at the downbeat like a whip, and voices surfaced from all octaves to iterate a taboo verse. (Did he say, "Fuck?")

The discovery of these throwaway wonders suggested something incredible about his already legendary capability. As more and more of his *Purple Rain* output took command with its subversive power, Prince drew his net tighter around the nation. His music was everywhere, and his influence was disconcertingly complete.

TRACK 5: "THE GLAMOROUS LIFE"

One of the most significant outcomes of the Sunset Sound sessions was an album for Sheila Escovedo, a young Latin with well-honed percussion skills. She was the daughter of a professional backing player and had been introduced to Prince by Carlos Santana. With some considerable coaxing, Prince got Sheila to take a stab at the mic. Following a first, successful collaboration on "Erotic City," Prince pulled her into the studio with a pile of his demos and completed an entire album on her behalf in just five days.

As with his other women, she went to market with a new name: Sheila E. Her album was titled *The Glamorous Life*, and it was "Jamie Starr's" third production of the year (under the banner of "the Starr Company").

Sheila rapidly became one of the central characters in Prince's career. She was his perfect model of integrative beauty. But in addition, she had talent. Sheila added live percussion accents that gave a new twist to Prince's electronic dance engineering.

Her musicality seemed to inspire other shifts as well. Two of the tracks he wrote for her (an album cut and a B-side) were entirely instrumental—the first such releases of his career. He also used session players to incorporate new instruments into the album: the cello, the violin, and—the real biggie—the sax, one of the only rock-R&B instruments he couldn't play himself. The title track of the album was the first cut on which he let a real horn take over for his cherished synths. It was a harbinger of things to come.

The album also reflected an emerging theatricality in Prince's work. The black-and-white album cover and the treatment of the title ("Sheila E. in *The Glamorous Life*") imitated a vintage cinema bill. Sheila was the "director," and her staff was the "cast."

The material on *The Glamorous Life* was surprisingly clean and straightforwardly pop. It pointed to a massive shift in operating style, but most significantly, the change reflected his apparent intent to encircle pop culture and make one last, decisive siege. As he'd done with the musical formulas of "Little Red Corvette" and "1999," he reached out to the whole universe of pop culture. *The*

Glamorous Life and its two single releases were 100% dance pop. Gone were the controversies and experimentalism. It was all listener-friendly hooks and verses.

The strategy worked. "THE GLAMOROUS LIFE" took up roost on the charts, peaking at #5 on Pop radio and crowning the list of dance singles. It was one of Prince's most enduring hits ever, and it became an immortal ghost in the halls of '80s pop. Sheila E. became a major star, and her success was another cornerstone in Prince's burgeoning empire.

With all these channels of output—Sheila E., the Time, Apollonia, his movie soundtrack and the B-sides—Prince still had leftover outtakes that made their way into the hands of other artists. One such beneficiary was Sheena Easton. Using the pseudonym Alexander Nevermind, Prince provided the British singer with a confection of "implied naughty sexuality"—a track called "Sugar Walls." The song made the Top 10 on both the Pop and Black charts and secured Sheena's popular success in the U.S.

Another monster hit was born when Prince lifted "Manic Monday" from his Apollonia work and gave it to the Bangles. Credited to Christopher Tracey this time, the track would top out at #2, blocked only by his own stalwart at #1 (1986's "Kiss").

TRACK 6: "GOD"

At the peak of *Purple Rain* hysteria, just four weeks after the album hit the shelves, the movie made its debut, and a premiere event at Mann's Chinese Theater became the inauguration of his Purple Reign. The audience at the red-carpet screening contained a wide assembly of celebrities, everyone from Eddie Murphy and Christopher Reeve to Steven Spielberg and Fleetwood Mac. MTV was there to cover the proceedings with a first-of-its-kind feature presentation that threatened to upstage the Grammy's as TV's biggest music event of the year.

Prince had achieved true crossover, and the critics were drooling at his feet. He'd crafted a mind-blowing album and devised his ultimate song. His stable of protégés was now fully assembled. Now the movie was about to thrust his swelling potency into the whole nation's lap.

True to its mission, the movie secured Prince's lordship. With long sequences of electrifying stage performance, patched in like music videos that supported the plotline, it provided the general public with a thorough review of his sorcery. He tore up the stage like no one before him, banging on the piano with his feet, jumping off speakers and humping the floorboards. With rabid sexual energy, he flurried through fancy footwork then descended into ball-breaking splits. He rubbed every lascivious spot and even wiggled his ass for the camera.

The movie also delivered some powerful image making. Thoughtfully calculated direction kept the Kid shrouded in mystery. He appeared and disappeared enigmatically and brooded in silence more often than he spoke.

Prince also crafted a rich depiction of his amorphous identity. He mixed frizzy hairdos and lace gloves with commando leather and chains. He wrapped silky white scarves around motorcycle masculinity. Part G.I. Joe, part fairy-tale princess—he was a mercenary of love. The crowds in the club scenes mirrored the multi-racial, multi-gender make-up of his band. Even the Kid's parents were cast as a bi-racial couple. (His mom was played by a white actress, perpetuating the myth about Prince's mixed parentage.)

By the time Prince rolled out a supporting concert tour that fall, he was the unchallenged ruler of the pop world. He even *looked* like rock n' roll royalty. Wearing Victorian prints, colonial ruffled shirts and a spangled stage coat, the royal dandy descended among his subjects like King Little Richard IV.

The five-month *Purple Rain* tour turned into a string of nightly coronations. The 100-show U.S. sweep was seen by almost two million people, grossing over $30 million and earning its place as one of the three largest tours in history. Throngs of concertgoers decked themselves in the hue of the Apocalypse, and the girls that were fully converted wore lingerie.

The mercurial talent from the big screen did not disappoint. The first 20 minutes were a non-stop thrill ride of hit after hit—the party to end a lifetime. Blazing white smoke billowed onto the stage, and flowers rained upon the crowd in celebration of the epiphany.

On stage, Prince went through a series of eye-popping transformations. He was a rock guitar god one moment. The next, he was swiping James Brown's funk and teaching the teacher how to really make it sweat. Ten minutes later, he was a half-naked, vulgar imp, twirling down fire poles, sliding across the floor, crawling to the edge of the stage on his belly. Three spins later, he was a blues troubadour at the keyboards, crooning in a piercing falsetto—a lost boy crying to be mothered. And he had a new outfit for every metamorphosis. (His almost-see-through lace pants were most memorable.)

The *Purple Rain* show continued to be driven by his sense of theatricality, and he directed the band to treat each section as if it were a scene in a play. The moody middle of the show was most unusual—and most critically offensive. During a long period of eerie darkness and sound effects with ghostly light, Prince openly acknowledged his moral conflict over the material he performed. He sang "GOD," an esoteric B-side that borrowed lyrics from the Book of Genesis, and delivered a penitent monologue.

A moment later, his shirt was off, and he was getting nasty in a neon-lit shower.

The final act repeated the storyline of the album and movie. The dark hole of "Darling Nikki" was followed by the spiritual pivot of "When Doves Cry." He was reborn all in white and launched into his redemption sequence, closing with "Purple Rain" as an encore. He and the band were joined onstage by a crowd of celebrants: opening act Sheila E., Apollonia 6, a couple of dancing security men and a parade of audience members. It was a jubilation fit for a king.

TRACK 7: "BABY, I'M A STAR"

From the summer of 1984 through the spring of 1985, *Purple Rain* was everywhere. The mainstream media was frenzied with rave reviews, speculation about his links to his protégés, and the delicious controversy over his brazen sexuality. Each element of the promotion machine compounded upon the others to create an unfathomable force. Videos promoted the singles. The singles promoted the soundtrack. The soundtrack promoted the movie. The movie promoted the tour. *Purple Rain* was a pop cultural phenomenon.

The album displaced Bruce Springsteen's *Born in the USA* at the top of charts and remained there for over six months, longer than any other record in history. It moved more than 13 million units in the U.S. and became one of the best-selling records of all time. He notched two #1 singles, book-ending the summer of '84 with "When Doves Cry" and "Let's Go Crazy." His movie grossed a whopping $70 million and ranked as one of the biggest films of the year. For one week that year, the Kid held the top spot on every major chart: single, album and box office. It was the only time since the Beatles that one artist achieved such a feat.

In the past year, Prince had manifested his personal vision more completely than a troubled, little black boy from Minneapolis could ever dream. At that moment in history, he was the most giant of giant pop icons. During his concert sweep through L.A., Bruce Springsteen and Madonna paid homage at his stage, providing backups as he performed the ebullient "BABY, I'M A STAR."

His ascension to pop phenom left an indelible imprint on the decade's culture. He was a new breed of rocker, a snarling punk on a bike with a penchant for rose petals and doves. He manhandled his Stratocaster but wore lavender high heels. His musical personality was an inconceivable conglomeration of ancestors—the tenderness of Michael Jackson, the flamboyance of Little Richard, the hyperkinetics of Mick Jagger and the grit of James Brown.

In the fulfillment of his vision, he led the campaign that authorized playful androgyny during an era of Reagan conservatism and set standards of style and behavior that were acutely individual in a time of stifling sameness. In the process, he fully delivered on his mission of Sexuality, pioneering new levels of acceptability from which the nation would never retract. By the time he finished slithering across America's stage, he had rewritten the *Male Guide to Copulation*. Striking out the chapters on boxer shorts and cigarettes in bed, he advocated colored G-strings and cunnilingus as an art form.

His ministry of sexual-spiritual liberation shook the spirit of an Alex Keaton-Wall Street world. Like Sly Stone and Jimi Hendrix before him, Prince promised more than just a rocking good time—he promised a higher plane of existence.

Of course, Prince made the most noise with his sounds, and in the world of pop, he redefined the meaning of "prolific." Over the past eight months, Prince flooded the market with 35 original songs and charted almost a dozen hits. It was a lot of new material for one record company. It was an unthinkable amount for a single talent scout, creative director, writer, producer, arranger, choreographer and multi-instrumentalist.

In the process, His Purple Highness shaped the sound of the '80s. The Sunset Sound sessions set the tune for an entire generation, and as a lonely teen had fantasized, that tune brought together the factions of a nation on one glorious, Uptown dance floor.

The first three months of 1985 were one long medal ceremony for Prince. America bestowed its gratitude and praise. In January, Prince received three American Music Awards. In March, he won an Oscar. And the year's Grammy Awards were refashioned into the music industry's official purple gala. Prince took to the podium twice for *Purple Rain*, picking up trophies for Best Rock Performance by a Group and Best Motion Picture Score. Then, just when it seemed his cap couldn't hold another feather, he was handed the Best R&B Song for Chaka Khan's cover of "I Feel for You."

That night, he capped off his triumph by performing "Baby, I'm a Star."

TRACK 8: "THE LADDER"

Prince knew he couldn't follow up the colossal success of *Purple Rain*. He didn't even try. Instead, he challenged his public with a confounding reinvention. In a series of commerce-defying contortions, Prince thumbed his nose at the "great follow-up complex" and again established self-guidance as his overriding principle. If nothing else, he would be an original.

It started with a stunning announcement before the last date of the *Purple Rain* tour. Manager Steve Fargnoli issued a statement saying, "Prince is withdrawing from the live performance scene for an indefinite period of time." That weekend's show, on Easter Sunday at Miami's Orange Bowl, was to be "his last performance for an indeterminate number of years." Fargnoli told reporters, "I asked what he planned to do. He told me, 'I'm going to look for the ladder.'"

Three weeks after the press conference, with almost no advance notice, a new album by His Purple Majesty suddenly arrived in stores. It was titled *Around the World in a Day*, and the keystone ballad was called "THE LADDER." In the opening phrases, Prince talked of an unloving, unappreciative king who didn't deserve his throne. The song was followed by a grinding mood piece ("Temptation") in which Prince played out the essential love vs. lust conflict of *Purple Rain*. Beaten and resigned, he told his God he finally understood the error of his ways and then advised his listeners that he'd be going away for an undetermined amount of time.

This, on top of Fargnoli's maddeningly oblique statement a couple weeks earlier, left heads and tongues swirling. Was the reclusive hermit returning to his shell?

If critics and listeners weren't confounded enough, the Prince of *Around the World in a Day* bore almost no resemblance to the star of *Purple Rain*. He'd reinvented himself as a psychedelic love guru, replete with finger cymbals and cloud-covered costumes. In previewing his new material for Warner executives, he showed up at the company's headquarters in a sari and sat cross-legged on the floor of a petal-strewn conference room.

The music on the new album was similarly yogi-istic. Delving deeper into traditional white sounds, he sprinkled his purple rock with a healthy dose of 1960s psychedelia. Many critics likened his veil of incense to the Beatles and their Eastern mysticism circa *Sgt. Pepper's Lonely Hearts Club Band*. Unfamiliar instruments, like the Arabic darbouka drum, spiced a brew that was uncharacteristically relaxed in mood and tempo. Another new element was the sax.

The album concept was a radical departure from the *Purple Rain* success model, and it was clear that Prince was cashing in on his breakthrough and buying a license to experiment. He refused to be pigeonholed and placed a premium on unpredictable behavior. Having won his commercial victory, he insisted on exercising his creative liberty.

Conceptually, *Around the World in a Day* was the rainbow after his purple rainstorm. The dark clouds of torment had blown out to sea, and sunshine and flowers filled Prince's heart. On "The Ladder," he celebrated the joy of redemption, the inner peace of his emotional springtime. As testament to a renewed bond with his father, Prince lovingly shared some writing credits with dear ol' dad.

A painting on the album cover depicted the spiritual theme. At the center of the illustration was a pool of cleansing water. A ladder of spiritual discovery led from the water to the heavens, and around the pool, all sorts of colorful characters gathered in search of peace.

Around the World in a Day seemed to be a dramatic moral reaction to Prince's four-year blaze of pornography-laced output and excessive commercial spoils. It was like he was shaking off the masses and moving out from the dirty castle he'd built with *Purple Rain*. His new residence was a spiritual retreat with greener pastures.

As part of his great escape, Prince had planned to slip the album out with no promotion whatsoever and no single releases. But Warner Bros. didn't follow through with the plan. Deejays had seized on the pop charms of "Raspberry Beret," and the record company pushed things along by releasing the single. "Raspberry Beret" and its successor, "Pop Life," both charted in the Pop Top 10. Those successes and the afterburn of purple mania hoisted *Around the World in a Day* to the top of the charts. It became the fastest-selling record in the label's history.

TRACK 9: "HELLO"

If sunshine filled Prince's heart, it was growing increasingly stormy everywhere else. The throne that His Royal Badness had assumed that year was already wobbling under his weight, and the first leg fell out within hours of reaching his pinnacle.

Following the American Music Awards ceremony—an event steeped in purple—the nation's musical superstars gathered in charitable union to record "We Are the World," the Ethiopian famine relief effort mounted by music industry leaders under the banner of USA for Africa. The historic assemblage joined the voices of virtually every contemporary pop icon—from Bruce Springsteen and Tina Turner to Stevie Wonder and Diana Ross—behind a Quincy Jones-produced track written by Michael Jackson and Lionel Richie. It was a shining event for the entertainment industry, one that warmed the world with its hand-in-hand harmony.

Unfortunately, the decade's new Prince was a no-show. His Majesty did not deign to descend upon the minions that night and instead held court with his personal entourage at a Sunset Boulevard nightclub.

By morning the press was thrashing his pomposity with merciless brutality. To make matters worse, Prince's security troupe had gotten in a tussle with some of the paparazzi outside the club, bogarting some film from an overzealous photographer. The combination of egomaniacal events ignited a public relations firestorm.

Steve Fargnoli tried to douse the blaze by calling Quincy Jones the next day and offering to have Prince lay down a guitar track. But the "We Are the World" producer declined. Instead Prince agreed to contribute an original song to the album project (a praise-Jesus epistle called "4 the Tears in Your Eyes").

In typically atypical style, Prince put out a P.R. statement on the situation, not through a spokesperson or press release, but through a song. The B-side to "Pop Life," entitled "HELLO," was a response to the national ego-disaster. His lyrical statement leveled blame squarely on a malicious media, and in the extended version of the song, he defied the press to walk a mile in his high heels. He went on to defend both his bodyguards and his record of charitable giving. (He'd funneled proceeds from the *Purple Rain* tour to local food banks and to a famously successful inner-city school program led by a Chicago teacher named Marva Collins.)

But the public relations damage was done, and the episode rocked his pedestal hard. On *Saturday Night Live*, Billy Crystal spoofed his egotism, singing, "*I* am the world," as bodyguards blocked a Bruce Springsteen imitator from approaching the mic.

A storm of public backlash was building on other fronts as well. At the Grammy Awards, Prince appeared more eccentric than ever, wearing a hooded, purple-sequined cape. Bodyguards surrounded his seat, sheltering him from the audience. When he picked up a trophy at the British Phonographic Industry Awards that month, his wall of security needlessly accompanied him to the podium.

The growing sense of detachment and arrogant inaccessibility was perpetuated by the difficulty of his new record; and his refusal to speak to the public or the media—once a thing of intrigue—began to feel petulant. Another shoe dropped when the *National Enquirer* published a major exposé entitled, "The Real Prince—He's Trapped in a Bizarre Secret World of Terror." It was based on an interview with Big Chick, who'd sold his loyalty for drug money and painted the boss' life as one of paranoia and imprisonment.

Along with Big Chick, Morris Day was also lost in the swell of *Purple Rain* success. The divide in his relationship with Prince had widened on the movie set, and after the L.A. premiere, Morris stayed in Hollywood to pursue a solo career. His departure provided mounting evidence of an empire collapsing under the weight of its ruler's overstretched britches.

With a whirlwind of negative press sweeping the nation, Prince relented to his first interviews since becoming a star. In an attempt to disprove the alien theories about him, Prince chatted with MTV and invited *Rolling Stone* writer Neal Karlen for a two-day visit into his private world. Driving Karlen through his childhood neighborhood, Prince was openly defiant about the media's portrayal of him. The article was a goosepimply brush against his not-so-thick skin, but at the same time, Prince dropped enough freaky notions and veiled references to perpetuate his image as an oddity.

The distance from his public was growing. Another nudge to the pedestal and his icon would be toppled.

TRACK 10: "PAISLEY PARK"

The success of *Purple Rain* had put Minneapolis on the musical map. Fans from around the world made pilgrimages to the local spots made famous by the film. At the same time, the allure of Prince's "Minneapolis Sound" fueled the growth of a vibrant recording industry there. Jimmy Jam and Terry Lewis set up Flyte Tyme Studios where Janet Jackson's rocket was launched. Other disciples like the Fine Young Cannibals came in search of purple-tinged production, filling the airwaves with Prince-inspired sound. By the end of the '80s, several of the biggest acts of the day—including Terrence Trent D'Arby, George Michael and Paula Abdul—succeeded on formulas copped from the Purple One.

Meanwhile, the King set out to build his own personal recording industry. Warner Bros. rewarded his success by granting him his own record label. He called it "Paisley Park" Records. *Around the World in a Day* was the first album released on the new label.

"PAISLEY PARK" was a concept central to *Around the World in a Day* and the title of a rock n' roll carousel tune that was a centerpiece of the album. It was Prince's metaphor for the long-sought-after mindset he'd achieved with *Purple Rain*, the colorful oasis that was depicted on the album cover.

Prince's vision for his new label was appropriately colorful, and he began assembling a label roster notable for its diversity. The expected label mates (like Sheila E.) were joined by new acts (like the all-white, all-boy pop band Three O'Clock), a first-time soloist (Dale Bozzio from Missing Persons) and forgotten veterans (like the Staples Singers' lead singer, Mavis Staples). His biggest signing was funk forefather George Clinton.

At a time in which Prince seemed to be seeking more spiritual comfort and personal sanctuary, a top priority for the label was the people closest to his inner circle. Longtime friend Jill Jones got some of his best outtakes from *Purple Rain* and a terrific album that went woefully unnoticed when it was eventually released in 1987. Jill actually had some vocal talent and had served as a backup singer on the *1999* album and tour. Her erogenous take on his "G-Spot" and ecstatic outbursts on "All Day, All Night" helped make her album one of the finest projects in the 10-year history of the label.

For some of the other pals in his camp, he formed a new band. Revealing a lot about the current state of his emotional needs, he called this cozy gathering the Family. For the cover art on their debut, he snapped photos of the group lounging around his home.

The group started with the last remaining loyalists from the degenerated Time. One of them—Paul Petersen (renamed St. Paul)—had taken over on keyboards and now found himself slotted as lead singer for the new group. The other members of the Family were, in fact, the family members of his tightest aides. The lead female role was given to Susannah Melvoin, Wendy's twin sister. Prince and Susannah had fallen in love during preparations for *Purple Rain*, and like all his girlfriends, she now graced the cover of an album. The group also featured a saxophonist, Eric Leeds—the brother of the *Purple Rain* tour manager. The addition of Leeds marked a profound shift in the course of Prince's work, throttling the horns up to full and spurring a new movement in jazz-funk fusion. (The group's new LP would feature two such jams.)

At the same time, Prince began constructing a sanctuary of another kind. Making an investment in his own personal industry, he commissioned the construction of a new musical facility, a recording and rehearsal supercenter. The contemporary, white structure cropped up along a country highway in an unlikely suburb 20 miles outside of Minneapolis. Built to His Royal Badness' own lofty specifications—at a cost of $10 million—his private musical-industrial complex included several world-class recording studios and an enormous soundstage for rehearsals and filming. The exterior resembled any other office-park building, but inside there was custom stained glass, doves cooing in a cage and a purple galaxy painted onto the ceiling of the boardroom. The recording studios were lined with granite, cherry wood and six tons of imported Italian marble.

In the basement was the underground vault that contained his legendary stock of outtakes. Hundreds of tapes lined the shelves of a climate-controlled and fireproof sarcophagus, duly protected behind an alarmed, steel bank door. The polished and professional facility also housed office space for his touring operation, his music publishing companies, his new record label and his movie production outfit. It even contained a full wardrobe shop staffed by seamstresses who made custom clothes for Prince and tour costumes based on sketches by the boss himself.

The facilities were made available for outside rentals, and over the years, the studios hosted a bevy of prominent clients—from Vanilla Ice to R.E.M. MC Hammer rehearsed his stage show. Burger King, Porsche and Huggies filmed TV ads. The movie *Grumpy Old Men* was shot on the soundstage.

The new facility brought the technical wonder of Sunset Sound to the quiet, secure environment of Prince's Minneapolis home. It was his ultimate tool of self-determination and creative freedom and the castle for his kingdom. It was a musical dream factory, a Fortress of Solitude that would allow him to eat, sleep and breathe his art. He called this heavenly place "Paisley Park."

Track 11: "High Fashion"

Flush with the success of his film debut, Prince quickly proceeded into development of his cinematic follow-up. His heady vision was a sweeping classic of a motion picture—a vintage 1940s-style romance—filmed in timeless black and white with the Valentino chic of a French Riviera setting. It would be a grand, influential art piece—a study in *haute couture*—and it would secure the mogul's position as a serious filmmaker.

Prince took up a secondary residence in France, popping between the south coast where he shot the new film and an apartment in Paris where he composed his music. (This new work was published under the label "Parisongs.")

Three new albums were born during this period, and each was drenched in Continental sensibilities. Two of the albums were protégé projects. The first was Sheila E.'s follow-up to *The Glamorous Life*. Just as the newly crowned Prince had wrapped himself in fine lace and paisley, Sheila was also reinvented in a more lavish, aristocratic form. The new record that Prince supplied was called *Romance 1600*, and it recast his leading lady as a 17th-century disco noblewoman. Sheila's masquerade ball was adorned with regal brass (the heaviest use of horns on any Prince project yet) and embroidered with love letters to Michelangelo. The power track on the album was "A Love Bizarre," a dance-club duet by the Lady and Prince that reached #11 on the Pop chart.

The most pointed definition of Prince's new, high-society habitat was his latest protégé group, the Family. Three of the leads were white, and St. Paul was the first Caucasian to front a Prince project. Even whiter was the unlikely sax man, Eric Leeds—a lanky, scholarly type who seemed strangely out of place in a Prince band.

In keeping with Prince's upper-class mood, the Family was presented more seriously than previous protégés. They were packaged as a proper gathering of chamber artistes. Photographed in elegant black and white, they looked like characters from his latest motion-picture vision, debutants of the 1940s.

The songs on their self-titled debut—almost all written and performed by Prince—were similarly austere. The opener, "HIGH FASHION," boasted a highbrow lyric that would have been comically cocky for the Time but came off acrid and arrogant with St. Paul on the mic. The rest of the album, including the lead single "The Screams of Passion," pondered the heavier side of love. The most dramatic moment was "Nothing Compares 2 U," which Sinead O'Connor turned into an international mega-hit with her tearful 1990 remake.

On the Family album, Prince dressed his pop more formally, giving it the mantle of "movie music." It wore a snazzy coat of jazz courtesy of Eric Leeds's sax and was draped in a shawl of orchestral strings. The string arrangements were overdubbed remotely by an L.A. producer and his 67-piece orchestra, and they gave Prince's music a classical beauty. At the same time, the album served as a prelude to a new line of snappier, classic funk fashions. (The sharp, put-together "Kiss" was soon to hit the runway.)

Unfortunately, even though it was a gem in Prince's crown, the Family project went nowhere fast. St. Paul quit before it could get off the ground. He was angered by the boss' stifling control. (St. Paul was forced to imitate Prince's own vocal style, and on "High Fashion," Prince even took one of the lead lines himself.)

When Prince began compiling his own album—supporting music for his new movie—his nose remained high in the air, and he readily embraced more classical, European textures. The cover of the album, entitled *Parade*, reinvented Prince in slicked-down, debonair style. As he'd done with the Family, he photographed himself in dramatic black and white. Tightly cropped hair, sharply penciled eyebrows, and a simple flamenco vest provided aristocratic flair. His pose—with arms raised theatrically like a conductor summoning a crescendo or a ballet dancer frozen mid-plié—completed the artistic presentation.

(When he showed up to present an American Music Award that year, his neatly coiffed look—almost radical in its anti-purple restraint—provided a delightful shock.)

By now, Prince's new releases were hotly anticipated for their certain surprise, and he didn't disappoint. When it was released on March 31, 1986, *Parade* revealed a continent shift of change, another supernatural transformation. The electric guitar—the instrument that had defined his popular success—was completely abandoned. Instead, the album contained the tight funk fashions he'd raised with the Family. Classics like "Girls and Boys" and "Mountains" were stylishly appointed with Eric Leeds' polished brass. The drum machine was also pushed aside in favor of acoustic skins, and the LP again flaunted his cinema-style strings. Stylistically, Prince flexed his abilities with unapologetic conceit. He wound his way from a carnivale theme, through a baroque piano concerto, to an Italian café tune about his boudoir.

One thing was certain: the artist critics dubbed the "Modern-Day Mozart" had deposited himself squarely in Renaissance land.

TRACK 12: "UNDER THE CHERRY MOON"

The cinematic follow-up to *Purple Rain* was called *Under the Cherry Moon*, and it was met with all the hype it deserved. MTV ran a premiere contest, and a lucky fan won a major preview event for her hometown (Sheridan, Wyoming!). With cameras trained on the MTV launch party, the whole world watched as Prince made his grand re-entrance.

Right there, before everyone's eyes, Prince tripped in his towering heels. The weight of thick hair cream and heavy cosmetics threw him off kilter, and his fragile 5'2", 125 lb. frame came crashing to the ground. The fall was in fact figurative, but the disaster that was his new movie was terribly real. *USA Today* warned its readers, "Don't even turn up on the same continent where this is playing."

With each passing week, Prince's career slipped closer to death as critics shredded the movie, screens closed rapidly, and follow-up singles bombed.

It started innocently enough—with an emotional storyline lifted from *Purple Rain*. A gigolo who worshiped sex and money (Prince's character, Christopher Tracey) and a wealthy debutante who worshiped money, found a better life in love. (In her big-screen debut, refined British actress Kristin Scott-Thomas played his leading lady.) The story ended in an "I Would Die 4 U" crucifixion when henchmen for the woman's disapproving father gunned down Christopher Tracey.

The problem with the movie was Prince's opulent decor. The movie's title track on the *Parade* album—"UNDER THE CHERRY MOON"—captured the odd mix of ostentation and languid emotion that marred the film. It was a poem scripted in sweeping calligraphy, but its verse longed for something meaningful to inspire it.

Like the latest trend in album covers, the film was produced in classical black and white. Chateau settings, eccentric costumes and pompous orchestration created an atmosphere of loopy pretension, and upon that stage, Prince put on an embarrassing display of narcissism. Banking on his fashion-forward icon to carry the movie, Prince mugged the camera and flaunted his newfound Parisian style.

His hiphuggers were decorated with gold lamé, and he wore more makeup than Bette Davis. Musical performance took a backseat to image.

As the world rolled its eyes, Prince documented an ego trip the size of Monaco. He spent gobs of money gilding his statue—almost twice the budget of *Purple Rain*—and took command of the director's chair himself. Without any oversight, it was a how-to video on arrogant self-indulgence.

Prince's celluloid train wreck almost snuffed his star out for good in the U.S. He'd elevated himself so high and moved so far to the white that he was disconnected from the street. Sales of his latest album only cracked one million, and his popularity was in rapid descent.

TRACK 13: "KISS"

The pulse of Prince's career would likely have flat-lined had he not given the world a "KISS." Nestled among the Louvre museum pieces of *Parade* were some funk masterworks, and "Kiss" was his Venus de Milo. It was the leadoff single, and it managed to get off the launch pad before the movie release halted his momentum. With its irrepressible groove mechanics, "Kiss" had no problem pushing its way to the top of the charts, lodging Prince his third #1 hit.

Unlike his other, more ornate work, this song—and its supporting video—was stripped down to its sexy basics. Prince's rhythm guitar tickled a throbbing muscle while his girlish falsetto danced on top. A quick smooch provided a fun hit of percussion, and the arrangement was appropriately pursed. The excellent video release was enticingly underdressed as well, and Prince bobbed and weaved around the stark set like a guitar lick in heels. Music and performance were back up front, and Prince's magic sparked again.

Another return to basics helped to sustain his impact. It came in the form of a small-scale stage revue, and once again, Prince's command of live performance secured his position of greatness.

Only a year after his proclaimed stage sabbatical, Prince returned to the performance scene with a series of one-off "Hit and Run" shows in the U.S. that eventually turned into a full-fledged *Parade* tour in Europe and Japan. The concerts were announced on local radio stations just a few hours before show time, and they were held in smaller arenas instead of the high-capacity stadiums that are the normal stomping grounds for a superstar. The excitement of these quick hits—coupled with the frenzy of unfulfilled demand and a pair of thrilling cameos at Sheila E.'s own shows—helped restore some of the lost luster to Prince's franchise.

The show was a stripped-down, James Brown-style soul revue—a fun-filled funkdown devoid of the recent morality plays and high theatrics. A horn section, anchored by Eric Leeds, was the featured attraction of an expanded Revolution lineup, adding a radical new dimension to Prince's showmanship and leading a pointed return to classic funk and R&B. Once again, Prince left his electric guitar in the case, freeing him up to frolic more playfully. Three male dancers in the lineup partnered with Prince on a black-and-white-checked dance floor, cutting up the open stage set with some slick choreography.

Coming out of a spin, Prince waved an instruction to the Revolution, marshalling his crackerjack outfit like a well-heeled offspring of the Godfather of Soul. During a brief break in the action, he kept the temperature high by seducing his microphone stand, dropping its imaginary panties to the floor, licking its loins and laying it down on the floor for a good shagging. It was a non-stop, no-frills romp—a wildly different show than *Purple Rain*, more at home at the Apollo Theater than in a rock arena—and Prince wowed fans and critics alike with his profound depth as a performer.

The *Parade* tour was Prince's first overseas appearance since a few *Dirty Mind*-era club shows, and the cities where he landed turned upside down with hysteria. The international press lauded Prince with the most hyperbolic praise yet.

Things were clicking again for Prince, and behind the scenes, he was in the midst of an inspired writing binge. Wendy and Lisa became his first real collaborators, spurring new styles and hastening his writing pace. They arranged the orchestral tracks, and with their love of the Beatles, they became muses for new musical directions. It was arguably the most vital writing period of his career, a marvelous period of experimentation and musical self-actualization.

As the wonder of "Kiss" promised, there were exciting things to come.

Playlist Three: Soulful
Struggles (1987-1993)

Track 1: "If I Was Your Girlfriend"

By the beginning of 1987, the music world was undergoing a regime change. The self-destruction of pop's Prince left a vacuum of leadership, and an uprising called hip-hop was gathering force in the streets. Run DMC's *Raising Hell* had just gone platinum—the first hip-hop album ever to do so.

As the sky fell around him, a wounded Prince retreated to higher ground, his safest haven: his musicianship. In a bold move that highlighted his one-man-band-abilities, Prince announced he was going solo again, and at the conclusion of the *Parade* tour, he folded the Revolution. Fans were devastated by the seemingly cavalier divorce from Wendy and Lisa, but behind the scenes, the oppressed girls were already plotting an escape. For Prince, it was an opportunity for another reinvention, a change in musical directions to build on the recent return to his R&B roots.

The newly independent Prince then presented Warner Bros. with plans for a monumental assault of personal artistry: a three-disc set called *Crystal Ball.*

Included in the set was material by "Camille," a new creative persona that he invented by speeding up the playback on his vocals. The plan was to market Camille as his more effeminate alter ego. With its helium-pitched voice, Camille was an effective masquerade for exploring the more ambi-sexual approaches Prince often took to bedding down women. These gender-bending come-ons were most persuasive on a new tune called "If I Was Your Girlfriend." A sultry funk drum and lilting synth line made a plaintive appeal for ultimate closeness, and in the closing bars, his desperate lyric swelled into a very hard sell. (He promised to kiss down where it counts.)

Along with the sheer audacity of three CDs—all made solo—the intrusion of the freaky Camille would inject certain interest into the new package he proposed. The record company, however, was skittish about the idea of releasing a high-dollar opus from a star that was drowning in his own ego, and to Prince's extreme annoyance, Warner Bros. refused to take on the marketing challenge of his abundant output. It was the first time he'd been flatly blocked from seeing a vision through to market. After bruising arguments with both Steve Fargnoli and Warner Chairman Mo Ostin, Prince eventually relented, but a permanent grudge had been lodged firmly up his ass.

The final agreed-to project was a two-CD set from the newly solo Prince—featuring a few guest appearances by Camille. The 16-track album was called *Sign o' the Times*, and it was a luscious cornucopia of all things Prince. It showcased his extraordinary abilities by mixing in all his pop charm and rock eccentricities (songs like "Strange Relationship" and "I Could Never Take the Place of Your Man") while bringing back some of his strongest R&B sentiments, including gospel, soul and cutting-edge funk (cuts like "Housequake" and "It"). It lamented social politics. It wrestled with alter egos. It celebrated God. It celebrated sex. But most significantly, it beamed with love.

It had been a long journey from the cold emotional vacancy of *1999*, but *Sign o' the Times* was unabashed in its expressions of love. The inspiration was Susannah, and the wedding theme that opened "If I Was Your Girlfriend" contemplated a real-life walk down the aisle. Susannah and Prince had become deeply involved, and she had moved into his new mansion near Paisley Park.

Each of the two discs closed with romantic vows. "Forever in My Life" spoke of Prince's desire to settle down, and "Adore" was a cathedral of commitment, with a crypt of soul and spires of arpeggios that promised loyalty until the end of time. Elsewhere, "If I Was Your Girlfriend"—one of the few Camille tracks to make the album—offered the same kind of intimacy that Susannah shared with her twin sister. There were also plenty of requisite rolls in the hay, but the sex was more devotional than animalistically lustful.

The first single released off the album was the title track, and after the loopiness of *Under the Cherry Moon*, its sober realism found Prince making a brief, thrilling touchdown on earth. The #3 Pop hit had all the funk solemnity of a tribal ceremony, and the royal chieftain spelled out his sage concerns: inner-city gangs, teenage drug use and one of the earliest artistic references to AIDS.

His visit to terra firma didn't last long, however; and when the single cover for "Sign o' the Times" hit the shelves, it provoked some concern. It featured a figure in a miniskirt with its face concealed, leaving open the possibility that Prince had gone drag. The back cover provided the punch line to the joke, revealing a new female protégée with a very Prince-like build—a dancer named Cat. All the same, it reminded his detractors of the threat he represented.

Popular opinion in the U.S. still held him out to be an oddball, and Prince supported those conventions with the release of his second single, the gender-warping "If I Was Your Girlfriend." Radio programmers didn't care to go there with him, and the single was promptly buried, halting the album's momentum. It took a classic American axe riff (the #2 hit "U Got the Look") to get things moving again.

Inspired by Susannah's muse, *Sign o' the Times* was rich with first-rate songs, and reviewers hailed the creativity. The album was a definitive expression of the transcendental fusion he represented—an amalgam of rich musical ancestry that channeled Sly Stone, Carlos Santana, Joni Mitchell and the Beatles. With an almost unearthly ability to adopt and assimilate sounds, he melded Hendrix guitar, Sam Cooke soul, Jackson Five pop, disco beats, Parliament funk and so much more. The album also captured all the dichotomy of his cultural forms—the black, the white, the male, the female, the pious and the profane. The album rocked, funked, swooned and punked, and universally, it received critical raves. To this day, many consider it his greatest work (among *Rolling Stone's* Top 100 albums). The high-quality material spawned three Top 10 hits, and the critical support kept his dimming star in the U.S. from slipping south of platinum.

TRACK 2: "THIRTEEN"

With the delivery of *Sign o' the Times*, Prince made a major retreat from the image disaster of *Under the Cherry Moon* and kept the focus on his music. Unlike his billboard-like portrait on *Parade*, the cover of this album showed almost nothing of the artist. Instead, the focal point was a stage set, decorated like an abandoned urban lot. Only a small portion of Prince's face was visible as he walked off the scene. At that, he was almost unrecognizable, wearing an Afro and wire-rimmed glasses.

For the release of the first single, Prince refrained from doing a promo video, and Warner Bros. released only a clip of some computer graphics. No images of Prince. The music did all the talking.

Part of the retraction stemmed from Prince's own disinterest in promoting the project. It wasn't the complete product he'd wanted to issue. And by the time it was released, the album's emotional muse had walked out of his life. Susannah moved back home to California, feeling something less than the unwavering adoration he crooned about.

When it came time for a tour, the show launched on the European side of the Atlantic, where Prince's popularity was still climbing. An album this robust required an extraordinary tour production, and in the short eight months since the close of the *Parade* tour, Prince managed to put together a whopper. A mammoth stage set replicated the urban junglescape on the album cover. It included chain link fences, neon signs and the hull of a wrecked car.

Like the music, Prince's new, post-Revolution band was notably blacker. The interesting new lineup included Sheila E. behind the drum kit (a woman playing drums?!) and a gospel singer on keyboards. A key holdover was the bedrock of Eric Leeds' horns.

Of course, the star looked a whole lot different too. He'd stripped the elaborate appliqué from his wardrobe and adopted basic peach and black as his colors du jour. At times, he got downright earthy, decking out like a New Age hippie in his spectacles and some tripped-out denim.

Prince's wide-ranging show was as brilliant as the album. The critic from *Melody Maker* called it, "the best thing I've ever seen…quite possibly the best thing I'll *ever* see." Returning to a more theatrical tableau, he opened the event with "Sign o' the Times" and performed a madly concerned guitar solo inside a solemn spotlight. Suddenly, the band appeared on the flanks, marching onto stage and beating out a military cadence on drums.

With that fresh reminder of the planet's demise, Prince launched another sexed-up sendoff. The show bristled with energy. Cat flailed wildly as his foil, and at one frenzied moment, Prince took a running slide across the stage, gliding between Cat's legs and snatching off her skirt.

The European audiences responded to *Sign o' the Times* with a fervor that matched 1984's purple mania in the States.

Prince canceled the U.S. leg of the tour when it became clear that the album project wasn't catching on back home like the commercial behemoth he'd envisioned. Instead of a tour, he did a performance on MTV's Video Music Awards and gave the U.S. market a movie version of the concert—mostly re-filmed at Paisley Park with interludes added for dramatic flow. It was a marvelous piece of film noir that the critics hailed as one of the greatest concert films ever made. Despite only a fleeting appearance in mostly second-string theaters, its strength helped to rehabilitate Prince's track record on the big screen.

On the European tour, the focus on the music continued with nightly "aftershows" at local clubs. Prince had begun this practice with the *Parade* tour and now institutionalized the late-night gigs, showcasing spontaneous set lists and intimately precocious funk. Prince used the forums to work out his appetite for jazz-funk jamming.

Prince's love affair with Eric's sax and a rediscovery of live instrumental jamming manifested themselves in a new side project. Over the course of 1987, Paisley Park released two albums by an instrumental act called Madhouse. The packages were curiously elusive. The first didn't contain any credits—no references or pictures of the performers. Nothing on the record sleeve except a buxom model. The track listings said only "One" through "Eight" and "Nine" through "Sixteen" respectively.

Naturally, the act was another disguise for Prince's supernatural output. Much of it was a solo effort, although Prince produced the project more roughly, creating the vibe of a live garage gig. After Prince had worked up a jam, he called in Eric Leeds to lay his horn on top.

The Madhouse project launched a heavy barrage of jazz-funk fusion, and with its shady origins, the assault felt like a musical Mafia hit. In fact, Al Capone could have been the producer. The tracks on the second set were segued with snippets from *The Godfather*, and numbers like "Thirteen" were riddled with the sounds of a stick-up. Heavy-handed jams swaggered across the discs like big-city thugs. They broke kneecaps without warning and sprayed gunfire without remorse. After a raucous getaway, they sat back to chaw on a thick cigar. One of the tracks, "Six," actually showed its tough-guy face on the Black Top 10 in spite of its anonymity and the lack of vocals. It didn't sound like Prince, but clearly it was the funk of a master.

Prince's move to jazz-funk instrumentals brought with it a new relationship with horn-blowing legend Miles Davis. The mutual admirers became close friends, and Miles shared the stage at Paisley Park and sometimes played Madhouse tunes during his own concerts. Unfortunately, a planned collaboration never happened before Miles' death in 1991.

Madhouse wasn't Prince's only ventriloquist act that year. He also delivered shrouded songs to Sheila E. and others. With a couple of his surprise attacks, writing as "Joey Coco," he showed up on country(!) records—with songs for Kenny Rogers and Deborah Allen.

All told, Prince sowed the market with almost 60 new songs that year—nearly double the flood from *Purple Rain*. Unlike that year, however, very little sprouted on the charts. The stream of projects taxed Warner Bros.' promotion systems, and Prince wouldn't stand still long enough to pay out an investment. With sales of his own project merely trotting along, Warner Bros. had little time or interest in plugging his numerous satellites. Marketing efforts were miniscule, and so were the sales.

Track 3: "Bob George"

As Christmas 1987 approached, an enigmatic new album appeared on the Warner Bros. release schedule. It was identified only as "Something" and was credited to "Somebody." The package being pressed at Warner's plants had no markings, and the sleeve was entirely black.

Another heavily cloaked Prince project was making its way to market.

The album had begun as a series of party outtakes, and much of it was composed while Prince was in a funk (the negative emotional kind). Following the departure of Big Chick and Morris, then Wendy and Lisa and most recently Susannah, Prince's support structure had been decimated. Now his artistic impact was in question, his sales continued to decline, and his own management had cut him down at the knees. With all that as the backdrop, Prince began to evolve the new album into a definitive statement of his funk authority. It was designed as a surprise attack that would reestablish his edge. The music industry adopted its own handle for the faceless package; they called it *The Black Album*.

The project was a pointed retort to accusations that Prince had lost his "blackness," and it sought to reassert his leadership in an industry that now swayed to the rhythm of hip-hop. Hip-hop had set a new standard of innovation—one that directly opposed Prince's worldview. Hip-hop had its mind on the street, while Prince had his head in the clouds. Hip-hop was an Afro-centric movement, while Prince lived in Uptown. Hip-hop was a culture of conformity—a fraternal order with uniforms—and Prince and his independent style didn't belong. Hip-hop emphasized aggressive beats and attitudes over Prince's seductive nuance, and it defined manhood at the highest level of testosterone, a level that reduced the tiny, fey Prince to a wimpish pansy.

Hip-hop threatened to make Prince obsolete. A prodigy's ego was challenged, and the pop Napoleon lashed back with an angry offensive. *The Black Album* was his resistance movement, a shot that would be heard around the world.

Reasserting his black power, it was a sweaty-ass-on-the-dance-floor record, completely different than the love-infused perfume of *Sign o' the Times*. With treacherous licks and grooves, it mounted the turntable like a mongrel in heat. Prince flaunted his mercurial talent with jaw-dropping jams, like the unusual titles "2 Nigs United 4 West Compton" and "Superfunkycalifragisexy." Discordant horn lines and sleazy guitar riffs added kinky juice to some of his most pornographic lyrics yet. It was the kind of funk freakshow only Prince could perform.

At the same time, Prince took jabs at the gangsta rap movement with satirical imitations, lampooning rappers for measuring self-worth by the price of their gold teeth. With a brutal dramatic pause, he commented that the only decent rapper was one that was "dead...on it."

Another hip-hop satire—"BOB GEORGE"—was his most hateful creation ever, a chilling flash of ghetto rage. Electronically lowering his voice to an unrecognizable, ghoulish basso profundo, Prince played the part of a murderous maniac intimidating his woman. The song's stalking bass notes created the terror of a dark alley, and his menacing voice reached out from the shadows like Death.

The name of the Bob George character purportedly combined that of Bob Cavallo, Steve Fargnoli's management partner, and music writer Nelson George. Both were critical of Prince's recent direction. The character was a vicious mockery of a hip-hop thug, and with it, Prince proved he could be the wickedest of them all—predating Enimem's witty, homicidal lunacy by more than a decade. After a cuss-filled episode of domestic abuse, the song ends with the sound of gunshots and a confrontation with the police.

One week before the scheduled release, Prince had a dramatic change of heart. On "Blue Tuesday," as he called it, he became highly distressed by the project's inherent negativity, its seething anger and violent tendencies. A new muse entered his life that night. An aspiring poetess named Ingrid Chavez met him at a Minneapolis club and slipped him a note asking him to smile. Prince took her back to Paisley Park where they talked at length about God and spirituality. Somewhere in the darkness of that night, Prince awoke to an intense anxiety about his new release.

The next morning, Prince mobilized his management structure to do whatever it took to halt the shipments. After a personal appeal to Chairman Mo Ostin, Warner Bros. began the Herculean effort of destroying cases that were already on the loading docks. At tremendous expense to Prince and the record company, half-a-million finished albums were pulverized.

Only a handful of CDs escaped the massive recall, and those that did became valuable collectors' items, commanding upwards of $10,000 on the black market. Within weeks, copies of copies were spreading through the bootleggers' network, and *The Black Album* rapidly became the most bootlegged record of all times. Its presence was so pervasive that the album actually appeared in the Top 10 of the *Rolling Stone* Reader's Poll that year.

Inadvertently, the withdrawal of *The Black Album* became a coup d' etat for Prince's aura. The thrill of the untouchable sent fans clambering into the bootleg underworld. To many, it spoke of his mythically prolific abilities. It was also a splashy display of his moralism, and it greatly amplified the mystique surrounding the dark side of his persona.

TRACK 4: "ANNA STESIA"

Within days of canceling *The Black Album*, Prince holed up in the newly operational Paisley Park studios, hard at work on a new project. The music he composed responded to Blue Tuesday with uplifting positivity. Turning away from the anger, it embraced a revival of religious faith and asserted his own musical direction.

Prince named the project *Lovesexy*, joining the sacred and the profane in a conceptual union of orgasmically intense spirituality. He staged the album as a theatrical event, producing it as one long, 45-minute sequence. (Unlike ordinary CDs, you could not select the individual tracks.) The whole affair became Prince's sacrament of confirmation, a reaffirmation of his Christian ideals. It was a revival party—with gospel wails proclaiming the glory of God. In a shower of spirit-cleansing redemption, tracks like "(Eye) No (There Is a Heaven)," "I Wish U Heaven" and "Positivity" all proselytized a more divine ideal. But with its intrusion of sexuality (race cars burned rubber in his shorts), it was a gospel according only to Prince.

The presence of his Blue Tuesday muse, Ingrid Chavez, could be felt throughout the album. She was credited as his "spirit child," and her spoken poetry opened the disc. Since their meeting that fateful night in December, Ingrid had become a guiding angel in Prince's life, and her visitation was recounted in the spiritual centerpiece of the album, a track called "ANNA STESIA" (from the Greek "anastasis" meaning "resurrection"). It began with hesitant, minor piano chords and a grim reflection on *The Black Album* and then built into a pious pledge of redemption. As the song structure reached a higher plain, Prince committed his life to God, and a choir of voices filled the score, proclaiming His glory.

Musically, the album was the pinnacle of his personal melting-pot vision. With layers of complex arrangements and dense production, Prince placed classical phrases over Latin percussion, piano virtuosity against James Brown grooves. It was an impossible feat: a symphony of funk. In an apparent attempt to reclaim his position as innovator, Prince actually labeled the material as a genre, dubbing it "New Power Soul."

Ever the antagonist, Prince devised an album cover that both satisfied his artistic vision and generated some much-needed controversy. The cover depicted the star fully nude, with one leg strategically bent to obscure the royal jewels. If you understood the album concept, it was obviously an image of spiritual rebirth. Pure and innocent, he posed on a giant white flower. He stared off toward the heavens with a serene, prayerful gaze. But for everyone else, it was just plain controversial. Many leading record outlets would only stock the CD behind the counter, and other retailers—Walmart and Kmart among them—refused to sell the album at all.

For Prince, *Lovesexy* was so personally important that he launched a massive international tour behind the album, including his first full-fledged appearance in the U.S. since *Purple Rain*. The stage set he conceived was his greatest spectacle ever. At a cost of $2 million, he built an enormous playground in the round, appropriate for only the largest of venues. The multiple levels held a basketball court and a swing set. The platforms seemed to come alive as whole sections shifted around on hydraulics and giant set pieces retracted in and out from the floor. As the show began, a full-sized '67 Ford Thunderbird circled the stage, and Prince jumped out to thundering applause. He was dressed like a cosmic Liberace—in the white, polka-dotted suits that marked this period—and his band wore boldly colored costumes decorated with playful lettering. Unlike the typical band setup, the players—including Cat the dancer and Sheila E. on drums again—were scattered all around the open terrain. Using mobile mics, they frolicked from one piece of playground equipment to another and danced underneath a rainbow of lighting effects like a street gang on Sesame Street.

The set list was divided into two sections. The first was a continuous, 80-minute medley of hits and oldies with a special emphasis on his more salacious stock. It got nastier as it went, and Prince strapped on garter belts for a naughty rendition of "Head." What clearly was the "dark" part of the show ended with a performance of "Bob George." As on the album track, Prince's rendition ended in a standoff with the police. He turned a gun on himself, and a shot rang out. As he fell dead, the arena went black.

When the light returned, he was reborn at the piano, performing his "Anna Stesia" redemption hymn. As he pleaded to God, the piano platform rose up, lifting him toward the heavens. Following an intermission—during which a reading by Ingrid Chavez invited the audience to "cross the line"—Prince returned for a homily on *Lovesexy*. Performing virtually the entire album, he turned the show into a halleluiah tent revival.

The album and tour project were paramount achievements for Prince, who realized an intense spiritual victory and new creative peak. But commercially, it put the nail in the coffin. The religious rebirth was too much for a public already dizzied by the hairpin turns since "Little Red Corvette," and his spiritual wrangling was too deeply self-focused for broad appeal. Prince was preaching a gospel all his own, and casual listeners had no hope of grasping his concept.

For the fourth time in as many years, Prince exhibited an outright contempt for commerce. First he'd thrown the world a loop with *Around the World in a Day*. In 1987, he'd quit on the promotion of *Sign o' the Times* then created and canceled *The Black Album*. Now, once again, he seemed to spurn commercial acceptance. His first inclination was to not promote the LP at all—no videos, etc.—although he later retracted. He did, however, move forward with a cover design and CD tracking (or lack of tracking) approach that actively worked against the marketing effort. Then, in the format and message of his show, he seemed to scorn his commercial past and deride himself and his listeners for ever supporting it.

On top of that, the idealism in his new music was no longer on trend. The racial divide in radio formats was beginning to widen again. With the advent of hip-hop, black music grew increasingly urban, and a new movement in suburban white rock was being born in Seattle. Times were changing, and the glitterati of the early 1980s were fading. Prince had ruled in the age of *Dynasty* and *Dallas*— embodying the vibrancy and possibility of a prosperous decade—but a grittier realism now seized popular culture. It filled the airwaves with grunge rock, gangsta rap and Alanis Morrisette angst.

Prince, meanwhile, seemed to be adding more crayon to his cartoon. His one hit single off the album, "Alphabet St.," had all the sugar-plum reverie and hopscotch butterscotch of a visit from the ice-cream man.

The music world had moved to a different place, and even with the benefit of his ninth Top 10 single, the album barely shipped gold. It was his weakest-selling record since his debut release. At several of the tour performances, the arenas were only half-full, and news sources reported that Prince's financial picture had big streaks of red.

TRACK 5: "BATDANCE"

With the Lord's light as his holy beacon, Prince was about to put his career on a steep trajectory of evangelical positivity, and the religious revival got started with a move toward gospel. Some of the first releases after *Lovesexy* were new songs for soulstresses Patti LaBelle and Mavis Staples (lead singer of the 1972 hit, "I'll Take You There"). They were his first female colleagues not to offer T&A as primary attractions.

Prince gave Patti an anti-drug, pro-love parable (the #6 Black hit "Yo Mister") and a space-age gospel rocker called "Love '89." Mavis got an entire album. The Mavis disc was a tragedy of opportunity lost. Instead of writing for her unique, husky voice and mature interpretation, Prince gave her Prince songs, and the results were disappointing. A much more potent collaboration took place in concert, when Mavis guested on the European *Lovesexy* tour to send up his unreleased gospel anthem, "God Is Alive."

The friction between his personal artistic vision and his commercial management structure was rubbing Prince the wrong way. So he once again cleared the decks of personnel around him. At the conclusion of the *Lovesexy* tour, Prince severed his relationship with his longtime co-conspirator and confidante, manager Steve Fargnoli. Within months, his publicist, lawyer, finance manager and much of the Paisley Park staff were also shown the door. Almost the entire backing band—including Sheila E. and Eric Leeds—were put on waivers. Prince was plotting a new path for himself, and once again the course would be entirely self-directed.

Prince was planning to take the year off to recuperate from the postpartum drain of spiritual rebirth and map out his next high-minded move. But a new opportunity presented itself. It wasn't the next step anyone envisioned, but it was too good to pass up.

Footage for the upcoming big-screen adaptation of *Batman* was being filmed in London, and at the invitation of director Tim Burton, Prince paid a visit to the set in January 1989. Burton hoped to get the artist to contribute a song or two to the movie soundtrack, but Prince was so inspired by what he saw that he pledged an entire album.

Returning to Minneapolis, Prince holed up in his studio cave, where he worked alone to prepare his snare. Two weeks later he emerged with a first-cut soundtrack to what would be one of the highest grossing movies of all times. Most of the material was surprisingly commercial—minimalist synths and drum machines that harkened backward to *1999*. The return to his cold electronica helped capture the mood of the film, but it also showed Prince to be playing it safe. In fact, this was the first album of his career that didn't hack away at existing paradigms. Nonetheless, Prince inscribed a compelling interpretation of the Batman drama and readily embraced the tensions of its inherent dualities. In the liner notes, he attributed the songs to characters from the movie. As "Batman," he opened the album with a "Sign o' the Times"-style commentary on the broken state of society, a song called "The Future." Later, "The Joker" stole the show with "Partyman," a featured track in the movie that boogied into the Pop Top 10.

The soundtrack closed with the summer's #1 hit, "BATDANCE"—an irreverent montage of disconnected beats and samples. Prince took the formula for promotional movie music and turned it inside out. Instead of writing a chart-pandering tune and then loading the video with movie clips, Prince put the movie samples in the song and made his own video statement absent of film footage. The lead performer of both was an identity that he named "Gemini"—a split personality portrayed by Prince in the video release. Costuming himself as half Joker and half Batman, he played with his own schizophrenia.

The song capitalized on the pre-release excitement of the movie by previewing snippets of dialogue from Jack Nicholson, Michael Keaton and Kim Basinger, while borrowing the harmonic "BAT-MAN" hit from the TV theme. From there, Prince went on a bender, creating a sonic mosaic of the conflict, chaos and sexual tension that colored the realm of the Dark Knight. Twice during the six-minute roller coaster ride, the rhythm shifted abruptly. Screams and shouts accompanied a scalding guitar passage. Interspersed were samples of his album work, all of which collided in a cacophony of sound.

As unconventional a sampler as it was, it did the job of kicking the Batmania into overdrive. The CD sold a million copies in its first week, returning Prince to the top of the charts. The success propped up his sagging post-*Lovesexy* finances and boosted his commercial inertia for entry into the '90s.

Prince's celebrity was rekindled in the tabloids when a romance with Kim Basinger blossomed from the *Batman* set. (The pair openly revealed their sex life by taping some icky bedroom banter on a 19-minute EP release of the #5 Black hit "Scandalous.") At the same time, his artistic stature was asserted by Sinead O'Conner's smash remake of "Nothing Compares 2 U" (pushed upon the world by her new manager, Steve Fargnoli) and by a number of decade-ending retrospectives that hailed his achievements. The BBC named him "Artist of the Decade," and the American Music Awards presented him a Special Award of Achievement for "influencing the look and sound of the '80s." *Rolling Stone* wrote, "Perhaps more than any other artist, Prince called the tune for pop music in the '80s."

TRACK 6: "NEW POWER GENERATION"

With the *Batman* diversion fully vented, Prince returned to his post-*Lovesexy* crusade. He'd put his own past, his management structure and support personnel out to pasture and was going his own way now—on a path of defiant career autonomy and counter-cultural evangelism. He gave his new movement and his army a name—"the New Power Generation"—and he adopted the imagery of a

New Funk cleric. He grew his hair long, wore a tight, wiry beard and put on a white tunic. He also made ubiquitous display of a new symbol for his Lovesexy religion: his famous merger of the male and female sex signs combined in a horn-like cross.

Prince put his mission statement into a battle hymn of defiance—"NEW POWER GENERATION"—that would bookend his next album release. Wielding a cannon of funk and the sampled sounds of a sword, the song blasted his detractors and commissioned his crusade.

In his first major project after *Batman*, Prince thumbed his nose at standard industry formulas and launched a new tour merely for touring sake, not in support of any album release. In another Europe and Asia-only affair, he mounted the 1990 "Nude Tour" with an atypically stark stage design and an exhibitionally broad set list. (The technical nudity also helped maximize the revenue.) The 56 dates—most in open-air stadiums—featured a new band that he soon dubbed the "New Power Generation" (or "N.P.G." for short). The new crew was more pronouncedly black—his first true "black" band—and included an Aretha Franklin-like vocalist named Rosie Gaines, a Minneapolis rapper named Tony M. and a massive drummer in African garb, Michael B.

Even without a hit on the radio, Prince managed to sell almost a million tickets in Europe. The acclaimed performance history of *Parade, Sign o' the Times* and *Lovesexy* ensured solid international support, and in London, his show sold out 16 nights at Wembley Arena, breaking all U.K. concert sales records.

Back at home, Prince was busy expanding his cottage industry—with an increased emphasis on private enterprise. He extended his commercial presence with the launch of a new nightclub business called "Glam Slam" (named for a track off the *Lovesexy* LP). The first location in downtown Minneapolis was soon joined by franchises in L.A., Miami and Tokyo. Each contained a private balcony with roped-off seating for His Royal Badness (including a cast-iron and velvet throne in Japan!) and had exclusive rights to spin unreleased Prince tunes from a stock of 385 said to be stored in his vault. Prince used the Glam Slam forum to stage his own surprise performances and to showcase his chosen acts of the day.

At the same time, Prince was rapidly expanding his roster of satellite artists—asserting command of his own personal industry. He orchestrated a reunion of the Time on a fourth and final album, *Pandemonium*, that brought back all the vintage elements—even the disguised Prince cameo—and yielded the group's highest charting hit ever, the #5 Pop hit "Jerk Out." Prince also handed out Top 40 hits to Martika (the 1985 "Toy Soldier" star returned to the Top 10 with his glorious New Age prayer "Love, Thy Will Be Done"), Elisa Fiorilla (a minor star who rubbed up against Prince while recording at his studio) and Tevin Campbell (the career of the 14-year old Quincy Jones discovery took flight with the #3 R&B hit "Round and Round").

There were several new Paisley Park albums as well. Withdrawing some unused Madhouse material from the royal vault, Eric Leeds released his own solo LP called *Times Squared*. Prince was credited for his contributions this time, and the few critics that noticed called it "Prince's jazz album." Another debut artist on the Paisley Park label was his Blue Tuesday spirit child, Ingrid Chavez. Hers was an album of poetry readings backed by instrumentation from Prince. It was an interesting experiment, but the result was dangerously spacey. Prince's atmospheric exploration of club beats and *Star Trek* samples didn't dock well with Ingrid's daffy recitation style and titles like "Slappy Dappy" and "Elephant Box." The most mortal embarrassment, however, was the Park's first hip-hop release, featuring a local unknown (T.C. Ellis) who tried to pass off a smoker's wheeze as rap talent.

All these efforts—the touring, the clubs, the spin-offs—reflected an increasing drive for commercial autonomy. In an early experiment with self-promotion of his private industry, he even test-drove a two-hour radio program called "New Power Generation Radio." The broadcast—presented by a local Minneapolis station and featuring new work from both the emperor and his protégés—was a telling symbol of a more self-directed vision for the business of his music.

TRACK 7: "STILL WOULD STAND ALL TIME"

For his own personal project, the high priest of funk had more preaching to do and scripted another grand morality play he called *Graffiti Bridge*. He conceived the project as a sequel to *Purple Rain* and wanted Madonna to play the female lead. The Material Girl traveled to Paisley Park for discussions but steered wide of any collaboration. (The only thing that came of their association was a Prince-penned duet on her *Like a Prayer* CD.)

In its next incarnation, *Graffiti Bridge* cast hot-and-heavy gal-pal Kim Basinger as the leading lady, and Prince brought back the director of *Purple Rain* as his manager and producer to deliver him his third big-screen release. But before shooting even began, the doubt-ridden manager quit the project.

Prince remained insistent on getting the movie made, and even after an ugly breakup with Kim left him without a co-star, he pressed on indignantly—slotting Ingrid Chavez into the vacant spot. And just as he did with his last movie disaster, he took on the job of director himself.

In a post-*Lovesexy* era of enlightened positivity, the concept of *Graffiti Bridge* was expectedly spiritual. It was a quasi-sequel to *Purple Rain* in which the Kid battled the conniving and loveless Time for ownership of the Glam Slam night-club. Meanwhile, the Kid has trouble winning over audiences with his soulful music and uplifting messages but is aided by a heavenly guardian named Aura, played by Ingrid the spirit child. Like all Prince movies, someone had to die for love, and Aura met her crucifixion on the bumper of a speeding jeep, delivering the Kid from evil.

Like its forefather *Purple Rain*, the *Graffiti Bridge* drama turned on a conflict that was semi-autobiographical. The Time performed "black" rap tunes, like "Release It" and "Love Machine," that the movie depicted as demonically sexist and spiritually bankrupt. Prince, on the other hand, was a misunderstood genius who found vindication in the affirmations of a higher power.

Released on November 2, 1990, the movie got a decent opening on *Purple Rain*-sequel hype and a personal push by Prince, who did his first media inter-views in half a decade (a second sit-down with *Rolling Stone*'s Neal Karlen). But ticket sales plummeted rapidly and screens closed within weeks, shutting down Prince's film career for good.

In standard fashion, Prince's drama was over-earnest about its significance. Coupled with a hollow execution—goofy writing, messy direction and amateur acting—the results were embarrassing. Although the performance footage was typically thrilling and the moody cinematography produced an interesting sub-terranean dreamscape, the sappy spiritualism and barefaced pretension drove the viewing public away.

In the big finale—"STILL WOULD STAND ALL TIME"—Prince pulled out the gospel and testified the Good Word from the preacher's pulpit. With arms flail-ing—halleluiah!—he proclaimed the saving power of love while a choir provided the praise-the-Lord backups. Run to the light, he beseeched the unwilling con-gregation at the local Cineplex. In the closing strains, the shadow of messiah complex grew longer, and a crowd of New Power Generation disciples held Prince aloft in a human cross.

The album that supported *Graffiti Bridge* was a spectacular achievement, a pop masterpiece jammed packed with some of the most consistently appealing material of his career. *Rolling Stone* proclaimed, "Prince crosses the bridge to glory" and marked the album's excellence with four out of five stars. The album was a mélange of diverse styles, made more accessible and credible by a stable of guest vocalists. (Among others, the Time, Mavis Staples, George Clinton and Tevin Campbell were featured.) There were plenty of potential singles, but once again, only one got off before movie failure crashed the program. It was "Thieves in the Temple," a "When Doves Cry" starlet that notched Prince another Top 10 hit.

The *Graffiti Bridge* soundtrack was clearly engineered for commercial success—as was *Batman*—and leaned on Prince's traditional sonic qualities. Instead of blazing all-new sounds, he retread a fair amount of familiar ground. For the second time since *Lovesexy*, his output seemed to be more consciously culled for its buyers than capriciously creative for its own sake. It had less of the self-assured spontaneity of old. With its astounding berth, it was a Titanic construction with something to prove, a showy extravagance aimed at reclaiming past glories. And for the first time, Prince seemed to overtly chase the trends that had gotten ahead of him, the trends he'd Blacked out while getting Lovesexy. Now he tried to assimilate the vocabulary of the age with lots more deejay scratching, sampling and even some rap.

Graffiti Bridge was truly encyclopedic in its scope—from the blues minuet of "The Question of U" to the rock delirium of "Joy in Repetition"—and it was clear that with the arrival of the new decade, Prince's latest strategy for asserting his power was to flex every well-defined fiber of his musical muscle. This new approach emphasized protean prowess over inspired invention. Unfortunately, as he increased the scope of his repertoire—test-driving more divergent styles—his albums wound up sounding more and more derivative.

The musical revolution was ending.

TRACK 8: "GETT OFF"

The commercial failure of *Graffiti Bridge* was sounding off alarms at Warner Bros. Records. Except for *Batman*—the success of which could be attributed to movie hype—Prince's last two efforts were moneymaking duds. The take from *Lovesexy* was embarrassing, and the sales of *Graffiti Bridge* didn't fare any better.

Warner Bros. executives pushed Prince to ease up on the pace of his output. They wanted him to follow the more market-friendly approach of other megastars like Michael Jackson, who only surfaced with new work once every few years. They suggested he take a break and cash in by issuing a greatest-hits package. But Prince wouldn't have it. He was driven to regain his status as a mover and shaker and had no interest in waiting. Furthermore, his contract with Warner Bros. would be up for renewal soon, and delivering the company a hit would go a long way toward maximizing his leverage. Without a manager to broker plans, Prince shut down any overtures of moderation from the corporate office. He was going his own way now, and he continued to dismiss any doubters.

He already had a new album in the works—one that would sail up the charts with "new power" positivity. The new release, *Diamonds and Pearls*, would reassert his commercial viability and give him the bargaining power he needed for the upcoming renegotiation of his contract. Warner relented, and the CD—with its bouquet of Lovesexy beauties (including tracks like "Live 4 Love")—took its place on the 1991 production schedule.

Diamonds and Pearls was just beginning the long march to market when, all of a sudden, Prince slipped a surprise into Warner Bros.' shorts.

In celebration of his 33rd birthday, Prince mailed out an independent vinyl "bootleg" to select clubs and radio stations. It was an impetus act—outside the Warner's system—that sought to show off a raging funk-rap hard-on that didn't belong in his now kinder and gentler repertoire. The outlaw release, "GETT OFF," was sent from Paisley Park to about 1,500 deejays. The yellow sleeve featured Prince's own hand-drawn artwork and a scrawled note: "4 those who think the little Prince is sleeping." The one-sided acetate contained a pelvic pump that slammed listeners on their ass. For starters, the sound was completely new for Prince. Featuring brute live drumming by Michael B., along with a Jeep-rumbling bass that was all the vogue, the track used vocals by his new band members and a slammin' rap by the prodigy himself. It started with a hair-raising caterwaul. Then the pounding bottom kicked in, and an Arabian flute theme charmed the mighty serpentine to life. With his hood unfurled and his forked tongue flittering with arousal, Prince flashed his naughty privates in a way he hadn't done since *Dirty Mind*. The song celebrated 23 sexual positions and detailed several of the less conventional ones.

The song caught fire, and the vinyl pressing instantly became a high-priced collectors' item. In an attempt to harness the illicit excitement for the upcoming *Diamonds and Pearls* release, Warner Bros. quickly mobilized to get a mass-market single out the next month and edit the album package to squeeze in the song. (The album was edited by removing a lesser dance number at the end of Side One, the title of which still remained on the final CD booklet.)

With the release of this one song, Prince turned his back on all that was Lovesexy. It was hard for him to hold back his primal urges, the lyric confessed, and Prince stroked the excitement that was reestablishing his street credibility and fueling a comeback. He produced a video release that took its inspiration from the porn epic *Caligula*, and it promptly climbed on top of the video charts. The video introduced the "N.P.G." and a new look for Prince. The color du jour was "chiquita yellow," and the style was "gangsta glam"—featuring pimp rags, "typhoon" hairdos, and costumes that spliced the DNA of Roger Vadim's *Barbarella* and Martin Scorceses' *The Godfather*. The video also introduced two new supporting characters: lovely twin bracelets named Diamond and Pearl that were the slampieces he gott off to.

Prince took the promotion of "Gett Off" over the top with a spotlight performance at the MTV Video Awards. Replicating the *Caligula* theme, scores of gold-painted bodies writhed on the stage in simulated orgy, and giant fire pots crowned a frame of Roman columns. The whomping groove plowed a canyon of sexual aggression, and just about the time it all seemed way too scalding for national TV, Prince whirled his backside toward the audience, revealing a big cutout in the seat of his pants. The ass-less trousers fed water-cooler chatter for weeks, and years later, the fashion police still recalled the trauma.

TRACK 9: "CREAM"

As the "Gett Off" exploitations demonstrated, Prince was willing to do whatever it took to make *Diamonds and Pearls* a success. Mounting his heaviest promotional effort yet, Prince did a flurry of informal sit-downs with reporters. (The "informality" meant tape recorders and notepads were strictly forbidden.) Several media types and industry bigwigs were invited to Paisley Park to preview the LP and watch rehearsals. Anthony Kiedis of the Red Hot Chili Peppers was one of the first witnesses to come down from the mountain, and he proclaimed that the new set represented "the greatest tunes I've ever heard."

The advance marketing continued with a plethora of pre-release performances, including a surprise, mid-day gig on the lot at Warner's Burbank offices and a one-of-a-kind mini-concert on *The Arsenio Hall Show* which was co-hosted by Patti LaBelle and attended by Little Richard, MC Hammer and other adoring celebs. Prince also did a string of pre-release showcases at key industry events. First he performed for 1,200 record company staffers in Chicago. Then it was off to New York to play for MTV employees. The following weekend he showed up at a black radio convention and staged a gig for the 4,000 folks who managed to squeeze their way into the Atlanta Hilton's main ballroom. *Billboard* magazine's R&B editor caught the show only by sneaking onto a service elevator and entering from the backstage via the hotel kitchen. For many, she wrote, the show "was a near-religious experience." "There is not one contemporary performer who rivals the Purple One in intensity, emotional appeal, personal magnetism, and sheer musicianship on stage," she raved.

Another signal of Prince's commitment to success was his hiring of Frank DiLeo as management consultant. DiLeo was Michael Jackson's manager and the guide for the Gloved One's *Thriller* and *Bad* successes. With the buzz surrounding "Gett Off," Prince had also effectively shaken the Warner Bros. machinery into motion, and the firm dialed up its promotional effort, which included several high-budget videos and an innovative hologram album cover.

Prince also did his part by delivering another highly commercial and accessible album. After a long string of soundtracks and concept albums, this was just a collection of songs. Prince came out of the corner swinging, and on the second track, the once-wilted warrior proclaimed himself to be "Daddy Pop." ("King of Pop" was already taken.)

The disc contained more ego-boosting than a Tony Robbins seminar (songs like "Willing and Able" and "Push"), and it was said that he wrote the first "official" single—"CREAM"—while looking in the mirror. The "Cream" single was released on September 9, 1991, and like the lyric chided, it aimed to "get on top." The classic cruiser grinded to a start like a sputtering Model T, then chugged off like a rainbow-colored convertible. With fuzzy dice bopping in the breeze, it quickly arrived at #1 and delivered Prince his 10th gold single and fifth chart topper.

As the *Lovesexy* revelation promised, the entire CD continued to soar through enlightened skies. Integrity and high-mindedness buoyed the disc, but unlike his recent spiritual epochs, *Diamonds and Pearls* was less overt in its religion.

Prince had honed the New Power Generation band into a highly disciplined force de funk and now recorded virtually all of his music live with the band. Just about the time everyone else had caught up with his use of electronics, Prince made things fresh by embracing Michael B.'s acoustic drumming. The hit seeker also produced the material with such friendship for radio that it was almost unrecognizable as his own.

Seeking to punctuate his unparalleled virtuosity, he reached even farther with his amalgam of styles, stretching the perimeters to their limits and staking his flag at each wide-ranging peak. ("Strollin'" was straight-up jazz.) In an obvious grab for hit value, he also added a healthy supply of hip-hop to the mix. Tony M. boomed in on half the tracks, and the Man himself busted several rhymes. Although no one completely embarrassed himself, neither Tony M. nor Prince had the gangsta rappers worried about their jobs. Compared to the high art form that was practiced in the ghettos, the N.P.G. came off as obvious pretenders.

The battle plan worked, and *Diamonds and Pearls* entered the charts at the highest point since 1986's *Parade*, eventually peaking out at Pop #3. True to its contemporary black design, it became only his second #1 R&B album. Of the five singles released, all faired well, and as his successes cascaded into 1992, Prince became the first artist in history to chart a Top 10 hit every year for 10 consecutive years (beating out the Temptation's 1965-73 string). All the hits filled up his wallet. *Diamonds and Pearls* moved six million units, and *Forbes'* estimated his year's earnings at $35 million, placing him third on their list of top entertainers—right below Oprah and just ahead of Arnold Schwarznegger.

Once again Prince had the world dancing in the palm of his hand. He kept things rolling with another overseas tour not seen in the U.S., another spectacle of unequalled proportion. It took 12 trailer trucks to transport a set that featured a giant Lovesexy symbol lighting rig and a cast of dozens. "Stunned and breathless," was one Australian critic's reaction to Prince's first visit there, and the *Melbourne Age* enthused, "There are performers, and then there is Prince."

Back on U.S. soil, the Sixth Annual Soul Train Music Awards were proof that Prince had won back his stature, particularly among his core black audience. Appearing on stage to receive a special Heritage Award, he was nearly vaporized by the blare of shrieks and screams. It took several minutes of halting speech to squeeze in a few words against the din.

Behind the scenes of public platitude, Prince was embroiled in yet another conflict with the corporate cogs. After being fired by Prince in 1988, his former management team—Steve Fargnoli and company—had sued him for severance pay as well as management fees lost when the star ignored their advice. In a separate legal action, Prince filed suit against the attorneys who represented him in the divorce with Fargnoli. The termination agreement had awarded "payments in perpetuity" to the one-time managers for any work created by Prince while under their counsel. The agreement gave the firm a cut of Prince's royalties ad infinitum.

Prince was deeply outraged by the notion of businessmen laying ownership claim to his personal creations. For him, it was another egregious example of the chokehold the industry machinery placed on its artists. In the name of young musicians everywhere, Prince's lawyers vowed to "help eliminate the widely accepted practice of paying management a percentage of an artist's publishing royalties." They added, "For Prince, this is not as much a legal issue as a moral one."

On the *Diamonds and Pearls* album, Prince leveled a biting commentary on the situation. In a rap that closed a track called "Jughead," Tony M. issued a warning to industry up-and-comers that "money-minders" were little more than blood-sucking parasites. Of course, the Jughead in question was Steve Fargnoli, and the ex-money-minder responded with another lawsuit, claiming that the public disparagement violated a contractual gag rule.

When the cases with Fargnoli were eventually settled, the payments in perpetuity remained intact. Prince had lost the battle. But he was preparing to wage a war.

TRACK 10: "GO GO DANCER"

The success of *Diamonds and Pearls* gave Prince all the leverage he needed for a renegotiation of his contract with Warner Bros., and he muscled for more ownership and control of his career. The final deal was touted by Paisley Park as the biggest ever—worth up to $100 million for his next six albums—and it drew a lot of attention for exceeding the recent contract packages laid out to Michael Jackson and Madonna. Prince's $10 million advance for each album was nearly double that awarded to the Material Girl.

The media jumped all over the announcement. Noting Prince's commercially spotty track record, the press soon found the catch that explained the obvious discrepancy vs. his mega-giant colleagues. The upside payout Prince was gloating about required him to generate sales of at least five million units per album. *Diamonds and Pearls* had just barely made that mark. Most other projects hadn't come close. If future albums fell short, his payouts would be reduced accordingly.

For Prince, the deal meant a lot more than money. Increasingly dissatisfied with the trappings of the industry, he secured concessions that expanded his ownership rights and opened new avenues for self-direction. The deal offered the potential for royalty rates that would well exceed current standards—rumored to be upwards of 25%. He also wiled his way into Warner Bros. corporate management, garnering an appointment as vice president in charge of new artists. The deal provided an executive office at the company's L.A. headquarters from where Prince could keep his nose in the firm's business.

Becoming an equity partner in Paisley Park Records, Warner Bros. also infused $20 million into Prince's label and created a second record label, named only by the gender-meld symbol, for Prince to develop new "street-oriented" acts. Meanwhile, the contract freed Prince from any promotional commitments. Videos, tours and films were explicitly omitted from the deal and were placed solely under his Paisley jurisdiction.

All of this was designed to give Paisley Park more autonomy to direct the careers of its superstar and various satellites. Warner Bros. executive Benny Medina explained, "To a large extent, his dependence on the big company didn't allow him to use all his talents. That's the spirit of this: given the freedom, what would he do?"

One of the first things he did was throttle the Paisley production machine into overdrive, dropping new tracks on anyone who'd take them. His work showed up on albums by everyone from Celine Dion and Joe Cocker to Paula Abdul and El Debarge. He also helped score a ballet. A new interpretation of "Thunder" from *Diamonds and Pearls* became the impetus for a full production by the Joffrey Ballet. The program, choreographed entirely to Prince songs, was acclaimed by critics and gave the company a big boost in attendance and exposure.

Prince's biggest act of self-assertion, however, was the launch of a new spin-off act. In a bid to retain his street credibility, he brought more rap into the Paisley circle. This time, his choice was an 18-year-old white girl from Cincinnati—not your prototypical rap star. Of course, that was precisely the point. Tara Patrick would be the ultimate marketing machine for seizing some real estate in the new hip-hop nation. First off, she ranked as perhaps the most stunning babe ever to enter his bevy. Her penetrating eyes and overflowing bust rivaled Pamela Anderson for drool-inducing power. She'd be noticed all right, and Prince would make his mark as the force behind rap's hottest novelty: a hip-hop version of Vanity.

That was the plan anyway. So Prince plucked Ms. Patrick from the dance floor where he discovered her, signed her to the Park, and promptly reinvented her. Like all obedient followers, she adopted a new name: Carmen Electra.

The byproduct of their professional and unprofessional union was Carmen's first solo LP. Produced and written largely by her purple paramour, it became Prince's first, full-fledged rap project. The album and marketing concept relied heavily on her pornographic curves, and the lead single was "GO GO DANCER." As an advance promotion, the song was sent to 369 gentlemen's clubs.

Unfortunately for Carmen and Prince, the release ran headfirst into a stripper's pole and collapsed. The project was a commercial flop—a disappointment that Prince again pinned on the ineptitude of Warner Bros.' promotion department. But the failure wasn't the company's alone. Prince's production sounded sadly imitative, and for her part, Carmen should have halted her musical career at the cover photo. In spite of what appeared to be ample lung capacity, she proved to have as little rap talent as the rest of the Paisley Park roster. Warner Bros. only sold a few handfuls of the CD, crushing Prince's hopes for hip-hop hipness.

The only good thing that came of the project was the increased visibility of Carmen's breasts, which soon appeared in *Playboy*, on an MTV game show, on *Baywatch* and at the altar with Dennis Rodman.

TRACK 11: "MY NAME IS PRINCE"

Building on the success of *Diamonds and Pearls*, Prince continued pushing himself and his work to the leading edge of contemporary black music, further integrating himself into the modern-day reality he could no longer ignore. He waded still deeper into the waters of hip-hop and contributed tracks to the latest album by Monie Love. He also re-styled himself for the age. He walked around with a translucent cane and a Tootsie Pop in his mouth. On stage, he used a microphone that was shaped like a pistol.

For his own next project, he produced his "blackest" record yet, adopting the full compliment of hip-hop and latest R&B design dimensions. The album's opener, "MY NAME IS PRINCE," pandered blatantly to the trend of hip-hop hubris. Prince posed as a braggadocio gangsta. Tony M. rapid-fired some machine gun rhymes. "Funky fresh for the '90s," yelped the new MC Prince, half shrieking the lyric over a steam-fired bass—his most bombastic production yet.

That hammer was followed by "Sexy Muthafucker," an advance teaser like "Gett Off" that was once again released on his birthday. It was Prince's first rap single, and he clipped his syncopated rhymes with a mouthful of attitude. The brazen use of the "f" word created illicit excitement, and with the support of a few deejays that defied a $10,000 FCC fine to air it, the single immediately shipped gold.

The new release was also hyped with a four-minute ad on TV in which Prince appeared as a darkly hooded deejay, mixing song samples on a turntable over a heavy gangsta beat. The album he previewed had a thick black current through it. Hip-hop guided the action, and when it took a break, reggae, R&B and church music stepped in.

The heavy promotion continued with another mini-concert on *The Arsenio Hall Show* and a network concert special filmed at Paisley Park. On the *Arsenio* show, he injected his own stylized interpretation of hip-hop, coughing up "My Name is Prince" while wearing a policeman's hat that had a chain veil hanging from the brim. Flanked by a hip-hop posse, he closed the performance by setting fire to a newspaper clipping: a negative review from Minneapolis critic Jon Bream.

One of his boldest and most effective promotional stunts yet came with the naming of the new album. It didn't have a name—at least, not one that could be spoken. He titled his 14th LP by his gender-blender glyph and offered no guidance on its pronunciation. The buzz over the unutterable title was pervasive, and it helped the album ship platinum. Along the way, it institutionalized his symbol as a cultural icon.

The other buzz on the project was the concept: a "rock soap opera," he called it. With the release, a new muse walked into his life and stole the record's heart. Mayte Garcia was a young beauty of Puerto Rican origin that Prince first met at a concert in Europe, and the sequence of songs and segues on the album told the tale of their budding romance. Unfortunately, the original cut of the soap opera was too large to fit on one disc, and some deep editorial slashes turned an oblique storyline into a conceptual mess.

Although it was completely obtuse at the time, the whole production was an homage to his new beloved. On the album cover, Prince and Mayte surrounded themselves with children, all of whom appeared in the likeness of his new lover. In the liner notes, Prince pointed out that his "mother's 1st name is Mattie." (As he would later reveal, Prince saw a cosmic connection in the names of his mother and his new girlfriend.)

The fourth track, "The Morning Papers," presented the pivotal conflict behind the opera's plotline and the artist's real life. As it turned out, Prince's honey was a teenager 15 years his junior. In weighing the public's certain disapproval, the song lyrics argued that age is nothing more than a number. As "The Morning Papers" suggested, Prince perceived the media to be his big spoiler. As the soap opera unfolded, a reporter, played by Kirstie Alley of *Cheers* fame, badgered the evasive artist about his involvement with the girl.

Mayte was trained as a dancer in Egypt and could do all kinds of tricks that Prince found fascinating: belly-dancing, sword-dancing and flipping coins on her stomach. Her muse—along with his own study of Egyptology—inspired lots of Arabian atmospherics on the new album, and to make matters of the Symbol LP even more confounding, there was a dramatic subplot running through the album that had "Princess Mayte" battling some evil Arabs over three chains of gold. The full story was told in a companion comic book, an appropriate venue for the nonsensical fantasy.

Exercising his newly negotiated rights for independent video, Prince translated the story into a VHS release that weaved the album's supporting videos into a short-form film. Without Warner Bros.' promotional support, the *Three Chains of Gold* video went largely unnoticed, but it was an historic assertion of his newfound creative liberty.

Track 12: "You Will Be Moved"

Racial problems in the U.S. hit a new peak in 1992. Gang violence had become epidemic, and the City of Los Angeles exploded in riots when white police officers unleashed their nightsticks on Rodney King.

A more Afro-centric Prince observed it all with deep consternation. He seemed to see the racial problems bore by African Americans as a reflection of an unjust system—not unlike the heavy hand of the white-dominated record industry that often held *him* down. Donning the poetic vestments of Martin Luther King, Prince wrote a political series that railed on the system and called on the black community to rise up for change.

A second album for Mavis Staples, entitled *The Voice*, became his most urgent social commentary. Using Mavis' rock-of-ages voice, he lofted a powerful and poignant plea for peace and social justice. It was his booming cannon shot through the noisy clatter of guns in the street. Making the most of their powerhouse collaboration, Prince created Memphis-style blues and Southern gospel forms that let Mavis' earthy voice shine. Her throaty delivery was the perfect vehicle for his plaintive appeal. On "YOU WILL BE MOVED," Mavis flashed images of the Rodney King incident and scolded the white establishment for their neglect of society's ills. Her powerful voice refused to give in to the degradation and offered God-fearing morality as the force for change. *Washington Post* critic Geoffrey Himes wrote, "In a year of blood in the streets, it may well be pop music's most powerful response."

The political series continued with compositions for Tevin Campbell and Earth Wind and Fire. On one of Tevin's salty teardrops, the young black longed to climb up onto Uncle Sam's lap like his white brethren. On another scorching track ("Paris 1798430"), Tevin begged to drink from the same cup as the majority. Moving closer to his own personal sense of discrimination, the track Prince gave Earth Wind and Fire—the brassy "Super Hero"—protested the disadvantaged state of black economic power.

For the next of his political diatribes, he created a side project around his supporting band, and he used this album to call the black community to action. In another bid for contemporary relevance, the disc by the "N.P.G." was titled *Goldnigga*, and it was a rap album, fronted by Tony M. this time and made distinct by the group's live instrumentation. The cornerstone of the album, "2gether," called on the gangbangers to stand up against a system that was stoking black genocide.

The *Goldnigga* disc was surrounded by its own political drama. When Prince handed it over to Warner Bros. to distribute and promote it, the firm promptly handed the album back. Concerned about the pace of his output and the project's weak commercial prospects (like his other forays into hip-hop, the disc was a soggy mess), the company slapped Prince with its first outright refusal.

Prince was incensed at having his social statement gagged and viewed it as nothing less than iron-fisted oppression. With a heightened awareness of the racism that ran deep in American culture, Prince began to feel its poison in the veins of his own life and career. His latent disgust with the music industry was evolving into feelings of full-fledged injustice. As he called upon the black community to change, he too considered ways of breaking his own systemic "chains."

These notions were about to drive him to a radical act of defiance.

Track 13: "7"

The biggest single off Prince's new, unnamed, glyph-marked album was the #2 hit "7," and when the video single premiered in late 1992, it seemed to portend some monumental changes. The song itself—a lush Persian tapestry of embroidered harmonies—was richly symbolic, detailing the drama of the Apocalypse as portrayed in the Book of Revelations. (Did the song also sound the death knell for the "Big Seven" record companies of the day—the all-powerful majors that oppressed his industry? Support for that theory could be heard in the closing line of the album, when Prince pronounced that his name would soon be "Victor.") In the video, Prince killed off images of his former self, and at the end, he and Mayte walked hand-in-hand through a hugely symbolic door. In his *Three Chains of Gold* compilation, the video for "7" was followed by a scene in which Prince shocked a conference room of Asian businessmen by signing a contract with his Lovesexy symbol instead of his name.

Several months after the release of the squiggle-marked album, Prince put a six-month P.R. event into motion. It started with a U.S. tour—the first in half a decade—that he called "Act I." The tour stuck to smaller venues that guaranteed sell-outs. Three dates at New York's Radio City Music Hall sold out in nine minutes. The lucky ticket holders included Whitney Houston, Spike Lee and Madonna. The show combined a greatest-hits revue and a run-through of his Symbolic rock soap opera, including some of his nonsensical theater about predatory Arabs and news reporters. Mayte served as his onstage foil, dancing wildly and making lewd display of her limber capabilities.

At the conclusion of Act I, on April 27, 1993, Paisley Park's press agents issued a stunning announcement: Prince was retiring from studio recording. The statement said he was turning his focus to alternative media—interactive technologies, live theater and films—and would fulfill his recording commitments with material from his vault of 500 unreleased songs. The move poked a sharp stick in Warner Bros.' eye, taking his career to the areas where he'd negotiated himself free from corporate oversight just seven months earlier. Instead, he left the company holding a bag of freeze-dried leftovers to dole out over five remaining albums.

An even bigger announcement came a month later. On his 35th birthday, Prince announced that he was changing his name to the unpronounceable symbol that titled his last album. Along with the press release, Paisley Park issued CDs with the downloadable font so typographers could reproduce his rune. The Park also designated an official spoken reference: "The Artist Formerly Known as Prince."

The news was met with incredulity and hilarity, and the national press went wild. Like all of his marketing maneuvers, the name change walked a fine line between promotional stunt and artistic self-purpose, but this time, the publicity trick backfired. Overnight, he tipped the scales on an already dubious public position and turned himself into a national laughingstock. Most of the world thought the unstable freakazoid had finally lost his marbles, and many translated his new moniker as "The Artist Formerly Known as Sane." *Entertainment Weekly* promptly dropped him from their annual list of 101 most influential entertainment figures, saying "Prince changed his name to an unpronounceable symbol—always a good career move—and announced he's retiring from new studio recording. And nobody gave a @#*!."

Of course, for the "Artist"—as he soon became known—the name change meant a whole lot more. It signaled a rebirth, a spiritual repurposing like Cassius Clay's transformation to Muhammad Ali and a libertarian revolt, the way Malcolm Little changed his last name to "X" in rejection of his "slave name." It was a clean break from his past and a teleportation to a new way of life. More than anything, it was a symbol of change, the currency of all great artists.

Giving up his trademark was a conscious career suicide, a forced separation from his historical successes. With it, he threw off the albatross of *Purple Rain*. Walking away from his brand equity was a detriment he welcomed. He'd be young and hungry again—with a new world of challenges. Under his new identity, he would emancipate himself from the white-dominated record industry and would attain a new plateau of God-serving love and peace with Mayte as his partner.

For a guy born as "Prince," the identity created by a name could charter a destiny. He'd reinvented the names of virtually every colleague. His own career had already existed under several pseudonyms. This then was the ultimate symbol of change: the jettisoning of a superstar ego. The new man would be a monogamous lover, a servant of God and a warrior for musical freedom.

"Act II"—a second, international leg of his tour—kicked off a year-long funeral for "Prince." In a totally revamped show, The Artist Who Killed Off His Former Self presented a hit-packed overview of the deceased's most popular tunes. The set list was derived from a fan-club survey, and it was the most slammin' memorial service ever given. The high-energy performances included some stage diving by both the Artist and Mayte, and the shows were often followed by lively "aftershows" at local clubs.

The London finale to the tour also served as a grand sendoff to his New Power Generation backing band—another casualty of his 360-degree reinvention. For their swan song, the Artist and his band performed three shows within a 24-hour period. The second was an historic live set on BBC Radio One. For the first time since Jimi Hendrix rocked it to the ground 25 years earlier, the Artist tore up an electric guitar in the BBC's prestigious concert hall. The midday, 20-minute firestorm left the audience and radio announcers babbling.

As the tour folded and a year of dramatic activity came to a close, the eulogy to "Prince" was documented in a series of greatest-hits releases. Doling out the first round of freeze-dried material, Warner Bros. issued three separate packages: one disc of "naughtier" hits, one disc of "nicer" hits, and a box set that combined them with a third disc of B-sides. In doing so, "Prince" became the first artist to debut three albums in a single week. Combined, the records shipped multi-platinum.

"Prince" was officially put to bed, and the "Artist" woke to an uncertain new day.

Playlist Four: Independent Crusade (1994-2004)

Track 1: "Interactive"

True to his professed purpose and principles, the Artist began 1994 by forging new models for his creative enterprise—ventures outside the reach and control of his corporate masters. He opened his own retail shops—the "New Power Generation" store—with franchise units in Minneapolis, L.A. and London. The flagship location, in Minneapolis' Uptown district, was part record store, part T-shirt shop and part museum gallery. The '67 T-Bird from the *Lovesexy* tour was parked between CD bins and clothing racks. Video monitors in the floor beamed rare footage, and a collection of gold and platinum records dotted the walls.

In addition to a complete collection of Paisley Park releases, requisite posters and key chains, the funky boutique offered "Purple Rain" condoms and a new line of perfumes, or "pheromones," each named by a Princely song title. For an extra fee, visitors gained access to an upstairs suite where rotating exhibits displayed tour costumes and the bike from *Purple Rain*. In a private screening room strewn with oversized pillows, they listened in on unreleased tracks fresh from the Park's soundboards and viewed clips from the Man's private catalog.

The NPG stores became a distribution outlet for several non-album—i.e., non-Warner—projects, including independent videos of live performance events and new photography and poetry books. A magazine publishing venture—a high-style, glossy title called *10,000* that promoted his cottage industry—lived on the shelves for one edition.

The NPG stores also served as the distribution point for his first independent album. In response to Warner Bros.' rejection of the N.P.G.'s *Goldnigga* project, the Artist defiantly created his own indie label—NPG Records—and sold the privately-pressed CD through his shops. That small stack of CDs, unnoticed by the world, was an historic event: a megastar's repudiation of corporate control, a Boston Tea Party to prelude a War of Independence.

Elsewhere, the Artist was trying to blaze a new model of direct artist-to-fan marketing by seizing control of the fan-club networks around the world. His "official" fan-operated club—centered on the seven-year-old, bimonthly *Controversy* magazine—folded in late 1993, and Paisley Park used its powerful legal resources to shut down the smaller national clubs. In their place, the Artist issued his own official *NPG* fanzine, which lasted in print for four issues before his fan operations moved to the Internet.

It was still the early days of the Web, but the Artist saw in the new technology an exciting opportunity for direct interactivity with his fans. An independent film project shown in the screening room of the NPG store envisioned this new mode of computer-based connection. Starring Nona Gaye, the daughter of legend Marvin Gaye, the 70-minute film showcased a collection of new songs and videos that Nona accessed through her computer.

A first manifestation of this interactive vision arrived a few months later in the form of a CD-ROM. The computer-based application gave the Artist a new multimedia palette with which to exert his creative vision and a forum to issue music outside the Warner Bros. system. Released on the Artist's first birthday (Prince's 36th), the CD-ROM and its embedded introductory song were titled "INTERACTIVE." The song began with the urgent beeping of an electronic alarm, waking his world to the new reality of Internet-based music.

The "Interactive" computer experience let users wander through a Paisley cyber mansion while searching for pieces of the Lovesexy symbol. Collect all five, and you got to see a new video. Along the way, you could climb into a deejay booth and spin records from his back catalog. You could enter his sound studio and try out the instruments, or go to the mixing board and engineer a tune. You could even frolic around his boudoir and raid his closet of tour costumes.

The release was celebrated by "the world's first interactive party." The Artist held court in Miami—at the grand opening of his newest Glam Slam—and his performance was beamed live onto screens at his L.A. and Minneapolis clubs.

Throughout the year, the Artist continued to experiment with new forms of live-performance interactivity. Mayte led a troupe called the ErotiCity Dancers that staged regular performances—interpretations of the Artist's latest music—at the various Glam Slams. A much bigger production at the L.A. club, entitled *Glam Slam Ulysses*, starred Carmen Electra. Built roughly around Homer's odyssey, the show combined live stage performance and pre-recorded video, all choreographed to 13 new songs by the Artist. On a large screen behind the stage, a beastly cyclops hurled boulders while a live actor bounded across the platform, defending himself with a giant Lovesexy symbol. Dancers in brightly feathered costumes posed as lotus flowers and showered the audience with spritzes of perfume. Reproductive mutants scrambled across the floor, and the video display showed an epic struggle in the club's bathroom stall.

The *L.A. Times* called the production "simply silly," and the Artist quickly shut it down.

The high pace of activity at the Glam Slams continued, however, and the Artist often took to the stage himself. At closing time at the Minneapolis franchise, he and his minders would sometimes circulate through the crowd, handing out invitations to early-morning jams at Paisley Park. In keeping with his kinder, gentler, ego-shedding mindset, many of these performances were benefit shows. With the ticket proceeds, the Artist donated equipment to pediatric clinics in each of the Glam Slam cities.

In a higher-profile act of charity, the Artist performed on a star-studded "VH-1 Honors" special, showcasing the inner-city school program led by Marva Collins. He brought the house down with the new rock number "Interactive" and a production that filled the stage and aisles with his colorfully costumed ErotiCity dancers.

Over the next two years, the Artist would center more of his activity on Paisley Park, perpetuating his own private enterprise of parties and performances. As testament to his more selfless, generous spirit, he inaugurated weekly "Love4OneAnother" parties at the Park, opening the facilities as a non-violent, drug-free "community recreation center." Making regular appearances to put on shows that were always intimate and often exciting, he seemed quite content to be the big fish in his small but self-made pond.

TRACK 2: "THE MOST BEAUTIFUL GIRL IN THE WORLD"

In a busy year of business-model making and breaking, the most significant event was the release of the Symbol's first single: "THE MOST BEAUTIFUL GIRL IN THE WORLD." The song was inspired by Mayte, and the reformed rock-and-roller celebrated "the kind (of beauty) that comes from inside." Although it wasn't widely publicized, the new single was, in fact, a major experiment in private enterprise. The song was not marketed or distributed by Warner Bros., which took a pass on volleying any more of his output at the moment. Instead, it was released independently. As he had done so many times before, Mo Ostin sanctioned the extracurricular action to assuage the impulses of his superstar. The single was the Artist's own first release on his new indie label, NPG Records, and was issued by Bellmark Records, an independent company with a staff of only 30. Significantly, Bellmark was a black-owned firm. With this high-wire event, the Artist was out to prove to himself, Warner Bros. and the world that he could succeed without the corporate machinery and that, in fact, it was the corporate machinery that restrained him.

And so, at the end of 1993, the Artist initiated a feisty promotion plan. Ads in the pre-Christmas issues of some national publications read, "Eligible bachelor seeks the most beautiful girl in the world to spend the holidays with." Interested parties were asked to send videos and pictures to Paisley Park. Then on Valentine's Day 1994, the debut single by the "Artist" was released with a video that presented the winners. Of the 50,000 entries, the seven who were selected represented a broad range of sizes, shapes and colors. Their beauty, it turned out, was defined, not by looks, but by their personality and dreams. One of the beauties featured was Marva Collins.

The launch date for the single and video was celebrated with an extravagant party in the early-morning hours at Paisley Park. The crowd of 1,200 invited guests included deejays and media bigwigs, celebs like Naomi Campbell and Salt n' Pepa, and basketball stars—Magic Johnson, David Robinson and Dominique Wilkins—who were in town for an NBA All-Star Game. The party featured a variety of "experiences." Eric Leeds presented "The Jazz Experience" in one room while Mayte conducted "The Dance Experience" in another. "The Live Experience" started at 3:00 a.m., and the Artist staged another interactive-styled performance in the Park's main hall. On a giant video screen at the backdrop, a cybernetic woman announced, "Welcome 2 the dawn," as the Artist tore into "Interactive" using a new symbol-shaped guitar.

In the days and weeks that followed, "The Most Beautiful Girl in the World" became an international smash hit. Held aloft by a heavenly melody, it alighted at #1 in several countries—including his first-ever chart topper in the U.K.—and at #3 in the U.S. It was now his 12th consecutive year of Top 10 appearances, and *Radio and Records* magazine named him the #1 most popular urban act of the last 20 years.

Most importantly for the Artist, the success of "The Most Beautiful Girl in the World" provided definitive validation of his anti-corporate position.

At about the same time, Warner Bros. shut down the hobbling Paisley Park Records label, but the Artist was granted a second shot at an independent release to promote his roster of spin-off acts. It was a compilation album—a sampler of tunes from Mavis Staples, the N.P.G., Nona Gaye and others—that was once again released on the indie NPG label and marketed and distributed by Bellmark

Records. The title was *1-800-NEW-FUNK*, the phone number for his latest direct-marketing venture. Through the toll-free service, callers could access product information from the New Power Generation retail operation, order his independent records for direct mail delivery, check on concert dates and enjoy an elevator version of "The Most Beautiful Girl in the World" while sitting on hold.

The *1-800-NEW-FUNK* collection was a solid package of promising material, including a third set by Madhouse and some crunchy pop-rock from a new protégée named Margie Cox. But in the coming months and years, the Artist never delivered on the series of new albums that was promised.

In agreeing to this second indie experiment, Warner Bros. forbade the release of any singles. But fresh off the success of "The Most Beautiful Girl in the World," the Artist was feeling his oats and made a strong promotional push behind "Love Sign," an undeniable pop duet by Nona Gaye and the Artist off the *1-800* disc. He invested in one of his slickest videos ever (directed by Ice Cube), mailed promo discs to radio stations, did a performance of the song on NBC's *Today* show and launched a promotional club tour called "The Love Experience."

Warner Bros. was less than pleased with his insurrectionism, and new lines were formed in the battle for commercial control.

Track 3: "Gold"

In June of 1994, the Artist appeared on a network broadcast of the Celebrate the Soul of American Music Awards, where he received a Living Legends Award. Rising from his seat, he carried a large pad of paper onto the stage, and after accepting the trophy from presenters Arsenio Hall and Patti LaBelle, he started reading from some notes. Speaking nervously at first, then becoming more assured over time, he delivered a lengthy monologue—more spoken words than most of the audience had ever heard cross his lips. He quoted the lyrics of a new song entitled "Gold," rumored to be his most passionate and majestic anthem since "Purple Rain." He concluded by thanking Mo Ostin for a "Beautiful" experiment and expressed the hope that his prodigious output be allowed to flow free. Picking up on the historic tenor of the speech, the arena's black audience responded with a lengthy and boisterous standing ovation.

The Artist was anxious to move forward with his own independent career—a more free enterprise that would allow him to accelerate his product stream. His famed contract with Warner Bros. called for him to deliver five more albums to the company, and in early 1994, Prince presented an idea that would fulfill two of these commitments simultaneously. He offered two completed albums and a concept for another "death marketing" event: the combined release of a final "Prince" disc and a momentous debut by the Symbol.

The "Prince" disc had an "implicitly naughty" title—*Come*—and on the cover, his black-and-white apparition stood before what appeared to be a cemetery gate. Below his name was the epitaph "1958-1993." The tracks inside all had one-word titles, and true to his promise, the material was pulled from his existing stockpile. Most of it came from his *Glam Slam Ulysses* debacle. Not surprisingly, there was very little by way of potential singles.

All the hits appeared on the companion disc—the first album released by the "Artist," a top-drawer set called *The Gold Experience*.

Fearing the over-saturation problems that their Artist so readily dismissed, Warner's management rejected the dual-release scheme, but did move forward with the release of *Come*. Happy to capitalize on their prized trademark, the company released the "Prince" album into stores in August.

Without its partner release by the Symbol, the issuance of a "Prince" album confounded an already confusing identity crisis, and critics blasted the whole mess. (The naming debacle was further muddled by another "Prince" product in 1996: the soundtrack to Spike Lee's *Girl 6* film, a compilation of several "pre-Artist" releases.)

Come had been clearly designed as a sendoff to "Prince," and the century's dirty little imp made sure to leave plenty of fluids on the sheets. It was a late-night romp under his bedclothes, strung together with interludes of seductively whispered poetry, all of which implied parallel dimensions of spirituality. On the opener, "Come," he tongued his way around the bedroom with nibbling horns and jazzy bites, and for the closer, "Prince" finished off his 15th and final album with "Orgasm," invoking a decade-old recording of Vanity having a toe-curling climax.

For his part, the Artist refused to provide any promotional support for the "Prince" project and, exercising his contractual freedoms, denied the company's request for any supporting videos. Instead, he threw all his effort behind the *1-800-NEW-FUNK* project that was hitting shelves the very same week. With little to work with in the wet and sticky puddle, Warner Bros. let *Come* dry up quickly. Sales in the U.S. of only 345,000 units made it the weakest-selling record of his career.

A bizarre squabble broke out in the pages of *Billboard* magazine when Warner Bros. promoted the *Come* LP with a pictogram-styled ad that gently poked fun at their Artist's unpronounceable name. The Artist didn't appreciate the humor and fired back with his own ad: a satirical imitation that promoted his independent *1-800-NEW-FUNK* release.

Meanwhile, discussions on the release of the Symbol's debut album grew increasingly bumpy. For the Artist, *The Gold Experience* was an urgent priority. Like *Diamonds and Pearls*, it was a top-flight collection of songs, teeming with potential hits—his best work in years, a certain smash that would snuff out the laughter and reestablish his authority. He'd engineered the album for commercial success, with a "Sexy Muthafucker"-like head-turner ("Pussy Control"), a puff of pop-rock wizardry ("Dolphin"), some R&B flamethrowers ("(Eye) Hate U" and "Shhh") and his new power ballad ("Gold"). The disc also provided a well-appointed home for "The Most Beautiful Girl in the World." Unlike the boundary-stretching contortions and black-trend chasing of his last few albums, *The Gold Experience* was a return to classic form. It was his most vital collection since *Sign o' the Times*, a critical and commercial sure-thing, a masterpiece that the world just had to hear.

The plans for *Gold* became convoluted by a boardroom shakeup at Warner Bros. following its 1989 merger with Time, Inc. A chain of management shuffles eventually sent his patriarchal anchor, Mo Ostin, packing, and *Gold* got caught in the breakdown. During the transition, both Ostin and the new management team tried brokering an arrangement for the album, and some new chips got tossed onto the poker table. One of them was *The Black Album*, and in a confounding swirl of deal making, the abandoned 1987 LP turned up on store shelves for a limited holiday release. Expectedly, it had little impact. As a statement, the idea had passed, having been played out seven years earlier in the bootleg market. Warner did little to support it beyond a half-hearted "amnesty program" that provided free CDs in return for the first thousand bootlegs handed over. Once again, the Artist distanced himself from the whole affair, saying in a press statement that he was "spiritually" against it.

After all the machinations, *The Gold Experience* still remained stuck in the system, and one of the biggest sticking points was the Artist's demand for ownership of the album's master tapes. Standard industry practice dictated that the record companies received ownership of the master recordings, giving the firm control of future use. For the independent-minded Artist, this was anathema to his quest for liberation.

Increasingly frustrated by his submission to the corporate system, the Artist started appearing in public with the word "slave" scrawled across his cheek. The unorthodox political statement was highly effective in raising the media profile of his struggles with Warner. It did little, however, to win over public support.

Feeling repressed by an upper white class of corporate "plantation owners," the Artist intended the racial implications of the "slave" brand, but many felt the analogy was misused. Others had little patience for the ranting of a wealthy prima donna whose career had slipped to the margins. Still others got the message, and contemporary artists like Master P got rich by clutching onto their master tapes.

TRACK 4: "THE EXODUS HAS BEGUN"

As the Gold War drew on, the Artist vented his aggravation in a press release advising his public that *Gold* might never be released because of the dysfunction at Warner Bros. With that, he launched a grassroots lobbying campaign that instigated fans to petition for the album's release. On December 13, 1994, he took the campaign to *The David Letterman Show*. An incredulous Letterman welcomed his guest with no name while displaying the new *Gold* album, which, Letterman reported with a heavy dose of irony, had a release date of "Never." The Artist then performed "Dolphin," a reincarnation fantasy about defying others' attempts to cage him. The surreal episode ended with the Artist feigning suicide.

The death marketing and *Gold* campaign continued the next month with an appearance on the American Music Awards, where he received an Award of Merit for "Prince's" contributions to American entertainment. Carmen Electra and his ErotiCity Dancers did a tribute choreographed to a new "Purple Medley" of the deceased's greatest hits. Then the "Artist" appeared on stage and proceeded with his own medley: a live performance of songs from the still-unreleased and unknown *Gold Experience*.

If all that wasn't bizarre enough for the viewing public, the show's close provided another inauspicious moment for the Artist. It was an awkward coincidence that the 1995 program represented the 10th anniversary of "We Are the World," and in the grand finale, Quincy Jones reunited the cast of stars for a live rendition. The Artist's participation was unavoidable this time, but he still managed to recreate controversy. As the scores of luminaries sang arm in arm, he stood on stage and sucked a lollypop without singing a note. At one point in the performance, Quincy Jones approached the Artist and held a microphone to his mouth. The Artist responded by thrusting his lollypop back at Jones.

A month later, the Artist launched a "free the music" publicity tour with a European concert outing that he called "the Ultimate Live Experience." He used the shows to publicly air the *Gold* material that Warner wouldn't release. Prior to the shows, he invited local journalists onto his soapbox and delivered lengthy exhortations from his dressing room about the broken state of the music industry. He railed against corporate ownership of artists' works and slammed the industry for segregating music formats through its promotional practices. Years before the advent of Napster and Kazaa, he foretold how the populist power of the Internet would one day bring the evil record companies to their knees.

For the tour, the Artist employed an outlandish stage design: three, large set pieces representing the male and female genitalia. The centerpiece of the rig, which he called the "Endorphinemachine," was a curtained "womb," and at the start of the concert, the newborn Artist was carried out from it on a conveyor belt. The enormous penis and vagina were logistical nightmares to transport and set up, and the shows were often marred by technical problems. Another problem in the design was the location of the soundboard. Seeking to direct yet another aspect of his show, the Artist positioned the sound controls inside the womb, and throughout the show, he ducked in and out to noodle with the levels.

The biggest problem with the show was the absence of fan favorites by "Prince." The entire show stuck exclusively to new material. While some critics praised his courage, most shared the disappointment of the audience.

The shows were also burdened by an abundance of political speechmaking. From the stage, he turned up the invective against Warner Bros. The word "slave" was a permanent fixture on his cheek now, and he often gave shout-outs to George Michael, a fellow "indentured servant" who was waging his own battle in the courts. The pallor of a ranting has-been kept the public at bay, and at one U.K. show, only 3,000 of the 10,000 available seats were filled.

The Artist also used the European tour as a distribution platform for a new satellite release: the second album by a restructured "N.P.G." (fronted this time by bassist Sonny Thompson). The CD, entitled *Exodus*, was another offensive in his war on corporate "enslavement." The Artist himself appeared on the disc, in the thin disguise of an electronically distorted voice and under the stage name of Tora Tora (a Japanese war cry). Dressed as the Tora Tora character—wearing a red veil to hide his face—the Artist joined the N.P.G. at promotional concerts and media rounds. In interviews, he responded to questions by whispering privately to Mayte, who would pass along the response. During these interviews, the Artist's language grew increasingly militant, and as he defiled Warner, his oratories on liberation began to take on all the qualities of a medieval religious movement.

With the *Exodus* project, the Artist hurled a pointed epithet at the industry goons, escalating his Holy War by waving a big middle finger in their faces. The "fuck you" missive included a blatantly "indie" package design, spoken skits that lampooned the entertainment culture and a live, P-Funk-inspired sound that defied contemporary formats. (He quit chasing hip-hop and reasserted his own soul-funk genre.) On "THE EXODUS HAS BEGUN," the Artist prophesized a day of reckoning for the corporate suits. Blasting out at the "spatch cocks in black face" that reaped unfair riches off the backs of artists' labors, he presaged the fall of the industry that would, in fact, arrive with the new millennium. The song was a ghetto-funk church service, and the Artist (as Tora Tora) preached his sermon while a choir rhapsodized his Good Word.

All the noise was heard at Time Warner, and a new management team tried to quiet the storm by providing the Artist a firm release date for his *Gold Experience*. The cease-fire agreement also included putting the N.P.G.'s *Exodus* on the release schedule, but Warner scrubbed that plan when the Artist refused to relent in his public derision of the firm. Hopes for peace were further decimated by Warner's refusal of yet a third album in the mix: an obligatory stroke job for his honey Mayte. (Her *Children of the Sun* CD was later released independently in Europe.)

The Gold Experience finally made it to market in September 1995, nearly two years after its original conception. By now, relations were so strained that neither of the embittered parties gave it much attention. Prince tried to create some stir by performing "Pussy Control" on the VH-1 Fashion Awards, using Mayte's half-naked body as his primary set piece. But in the end, only one single (the #3 R&B hit "(Eye) Hate U") received any notice, and the once-landmark debut by the Symbol came and went from the charts in a short eight weeks.

By the end of 1995, the Artist was in deep distress. His "shackles" weighed heavy on his spirit and on his career, and his finances were in shambles. He severed all ties to Los Angeles—the seat of the evil corporate empire—selling his Bel Air home and his local Glam Slam. Additional cost-cutting soon shuttered the other Glam Slams and the NPG stores.

On December 22, 1995, he ended a troubled year with another press statement. It announced that he had "officially given notice to Warner Bros. Records of his desire to terminate his recording agreement."

TRACK 5: "BETCHA BY GOLLY WOW"

The New Year brought sunnier skies for the Artist. On Valentine's Day 1996, he married Mayte in a small ceremony at a Minneapolis church (the same hometown hall where he'd played ball as a kid), and the happy couple wasted no time building their family. Two months after the wedding, an official press release gushed that Mayte was pregnant.

The joy of having a family transformed the Artist and brightened the halls of Paisley Park. Closing the facility as a rental operation, he and Mayte remodeled the Park into a romper land. They painted clouds onto the walls of the atrium and built a nursery near the Artist's studio and a playground out back. Together they began work on a children's book and companion CD. The giddy father-to-be even made a guest appearance on *The Muppets* TV show.

At the same time, the Artist's career began to emerge from its long winter. On his wedding day, he launched the Internet operation that would define his future, creating the direct, unhindered conduit that, he believed, would revolutionize the industry and his own creative enterprise. The new website, called the Dawn, was one of the first online franchises by an artist (David Bowie was another prominent pioneer), and it offered snippets of unreleased songs along with news updates and a bulletin board for the Artist's socio-political editorials. (At its launch, the website posted his wedding program, which presented a mystical perspective on his union with Mayte.)

Good progress was also being made in the divorce from Time Warner, and a new legal representative—a young, black lawyer named Londell McMillan—took advantage of yet another management rotation at the company's troubled headquarters. With its corporate house in disarray, the firm decided it could no longer afford the Artist's P.R. grief, and a deal was cut to give him an early out on his contract. In return for taking a sizeable reduction in royalty advances, McMillan arranged for the simultaneous delivery of two final albums.

With no hesitation, the Artist slopped together the two discs that would set him free. Both drew primarily on material from his vault, and most of it was the kind of facile workouts he could do in his sleep—material that seemed deliberately weak. The first record—entitled *Chaos and Disorder*—was heavy on rock and blues, while the second—*The Vault: Old Friends 4 Sale*—sang its blues with more jazz. Both were short, uninspired essays—obligations designed to meet the minimum requirement—and both contained some bitter flavors. The cover of *Chaos and Disorder* depicted a syringe filled with money and a military boot print on a broken record. With his other final handoff, he forced Warner to go to market with a title (*Old Friends 4 Sale*) that laid bare the acrimony in surrendering his works.

When released—*Chaos* in July and *The Vault* three years later—nobody gave them much support. Prince made a couple of showings to promote *Chaos and Disorder*, but the performances felt as forced as they were. The only sign of passion from the begrudging pitchman, who still wore the "slave" brand on his face, came on *The David Letterman Show*, when he gave the shout-out, "Free T.L.C." (The hip-hop-soul trio was in bankruptcy despite chart-topping sales.)

The Artist hardly noticed the new lows in his sales figures. The war was over. At last, he was free.

The Artist's plan for marking his freedom from Warner Bros. involved a monster assertion of his creative authority: a three-CD set like the *Crystal Ball* package the company had rejected 10 years earlier. It would be titled *Emancipation*.

The Artist did virtually all recording for the project on his own, taking his inspiration from the bliss of marriage and the expectation of fatherhood. His emotional rapture was captured in the unexpected cover of an old Stylistics song: "BETCHA BY GOLLY WOW." Of his new wife and new life, he gushed that all his fairy tales were coming true.

Most other tracks for the album followed suit, swooning with love (like "Soul Sanctuary" and "Friend, Lover, Sister, Mother/Wife") and anticipating the arrival of his baby. One song used a sonogram of the baby's heartbeat as its rhythm line. The CD artwork showed Mayte's pregnant belly and what appeared to be an ultrasound image of the unborn child.

Holding himself to an ambitious schedule, the Artist targeted the release of the new project—the rebirth of his career—to coincide with the birth of his baby in early November.

The finished work was a Herculean achievement, purportedly the longest recording of new material every produced. Using the lofty specifications of the Egyptian pyramids as his guide, the Artist arranged the 36 songs into three CDs, each containing 12 tracks and running exactly one hour. Despite its gargantuan proportions and another big stretch of stylistic aerobics (from jump jazz to techno house), the underlying emotion provided cohesion, and the wellspring of inspiration kept the quality level high for the entire three hours. As with his other recent releases, there was nothing really new in the musical vocabulary, but his writing benefited from a relaxed happiness and confident maturity.

The biggest missteps on the album were politically motivated. He deliberately thwarted potential hits (like "The Holy River") by refusing to edit his muse, as Warner Bros. would have done. He also missed the mark on a couple of weak cover tunes that were only there to yield royalties for some retired "slaves."

To maximize the promotional effort behind *Emancipation*, the Artist sought out a one-album deal for marketing and distributing the project through one of the major record companies. Londell McMillan led the negotiations and landed a deal with EMI that met all the artist's demands. EMI would handle manufacturing, distribution and promotion, but the Artist called all the shots. He had no commitments to EMI beyond the one record, and he owned the master tapes and reaped the lion's share of the profits. It was a revolutionary deal for an artist of his caliber.

The marketing effort was thrown into high gear, and on November 12, 1996, Paisley Park hosted a celebration of "Freedom Day." The Artist performed a 25-minute concert on his soundstage that was carried live by MTV, VH-1 and BET. It opened with a tape of Martin Luther King's famous oratory—"Free at last, free at last. Thank God Almighty, we're free at last"—as laser lights beamed "Emancipation" across the scrim.

Immediately following the show, the Artist held audience in a studio with the more than 100 reporters who'd gathered for this auspicious moment in music history. The next morning saw the broad-scale release of a first single, "Betcha By Golly Wow," and a supporting video that celebrated Mayte's pregnancy.

A week later, the massive *Emancipation* box hit with more positive attention than any project since *Diamonds and Pearls*. Critics hailed his achievement, and the album darted to #11 on the Pop chart—a credible peak for a high-dollar, multi-disc set. As the shipments climbed toward double-platinum status (the triple set required only 666,000 units to hit the mark), EMI arranged a celebratory party in New York that attracted everyone from L.L. Cool J and Chris Rock to Marilyn Manson, Peter Gabriel and the Smashing Pumpkins.

For the moment, the Artist was making an impact again. He'd polished his crown and reclaimed some commercial success. And most significantly, he'd done it all his own way: all on his own. One of his greatest sources of pride and satisfaction was the pile of cash that rapidly mounted. With only a fraction of the units, his bankroll from *Emancipation* eclipsed that of *Purple Rain*.

TRACK 6: "COMEBACK"

Behind the face of public success, the Artist was living a nightmare. As his career rebirth was rolling off the production lines, the birth of his cherished baby turned tragic. On October 16, 1996, Mayte gave birth to a son, but the premature boy was born with a severe deformity of the skull—the cruel result of a genetic disorder called Pfeiffer's Syndrome. The baby was unlikely to survive. He was in pain and underwent surgery twice in his first week of life. At the same time that EMI was revving up for a "celebration of life, love and liberty" (as *Emancipation* was headlined), the Artist and Mayte made the decision to let their baby die.

The infant son had been deceased for only three weeks when the Artist took to the stage on "Freedom Day."

In the midst of unthinkable horror, the Artist went on with the locked-and-loaded promotions for *Emancipation*, which called for the most extensive interview circuit of his career. To symbolize a new period of change and openness, he was booked for several TV sit-downs. The first in his career—an hour-long event on *The Oprah Winfrey Show*—occurred just weeks after his baby's death. The Artist was desperate to keep the matter private and enforced a legal gag order on knowing aides; but some of the tabloids picked up on the story, prompting Oprah to gently probe. The Artist gave her a non-answer and quickly put up his well-developed screen.

Many more televised appearances followed, including an interview with comedian Chris Rock on VH-1 and a visit to *The Rosie O'Donnell Show*. The Artist's first-ever live TV chat took place on NBC's *Today* show with Bryant Gumble. Again, the baby's death provided an awkward and tragic backdrop. Mayte joined him and looked down at the floor in silence when Gumble inquired about their baby. The focus on *Emancipation* was quickly waning.

The Artist continued promoting the project—with a performance of the title track at the NAACP Image Awards (rousing the African-American audience by breaking out of manacles) and with a return visit to the *Today* show. There he did an amiable roast for the departing Bryant Gumble, imitating his dress and mannerisms with a customized take on "Raspberry Beret." In all of it, however, there was little focus on the new album. Instead, the attention centered on the Artist's personal affairs: his feud with Warner Bros., the lingering joke that was his name, his marriage to Mayte…and the death of his son.

Other factors conspired to cause a premature demise of the *Emancipation* project and the Artist's career comeback. His independent choice of singles proved to be misguided. He thought the inclusion of cover songs would generate some interest; however, the personally meaningful but culturally irrelevant "Betcha By Golly Wow" went nowhere. Then, as the second single was being released, EMI shut down its music division due to financial problems, and the company's promotional operations immediately withered.

The Artist took that occasion to walk away from *Emancipation* and all its emotional associations.

Back in the quiet of Paisley Park, he contemplated recent events on a quiet recording that eventually saw a quiet release in 1998. It was his first unplugged album, an acoustic guitar project. Deep within *The Truth*, as he called his stripped-down recording, he issued the only song that can be clearly seen as a reflection on the loss of his son, a eulogy called "COMEBACK." Singing quietly over melancholy, almost numbly rhythmic strumming, the Artist described feeling a breeze blow as his loved one's soul passed by. At the end of the song, his vocals made an unexpected break into a multi-part harmony, picking up a Beatles-like chorus that grasped for hope of a future reunion, before the mix dropped back to sad, contemplative guitar picking. In the somber coda, he verbalized a musical instruction: "Tears go here."

A year later, there would be another casualty in his life. The Artist and Mayte announced the annulment of their marriage, ostensibly because of a newfound abhorrence of contracts. But it was soon clear that the grounds for the separation ran much deeper—all the way back, certainly, to the pain they'd suffered with the death of their son. In 1999, the couple parted ways. In both his family life and his career, the 40-year-old Artist died an untimely death.

TRACK 7: "DON'T PLAY ME"

Following the collapse of *Emancipation*, the Artist turned inward with his artistic enterprise. Several months later, he went forward with a planned *Emancipation* tour in the U.S. but reconceived it for new purposes. He called the first leg the "Love4OneAnother Charities Tour," and it became a funding source for a new philanthropic enterprise at Paisley Park. The proceeds were quietly funneled to the support of children's medical services.

The rest of the 65-date run—the most extensive since *Purple Rain*—was known as "The Jam of the Year," and it was a new exercise in commercial independence. Paisley Park planned and executed each tour date autonomously—without the intermediary support of promoters or booking agents. Staffers scheduled the venues just weeks before the show and coordinated the local market promotions. In an effort to thwart scalpers from profiting off the shows, tickets went on sale just days in advance. Even still, the Artist managed to draw credible crowds—often in smaller cities where he'd never appeared before. Mixing the hits with top-drawer novelties, the concerts received positive reviews. But once again, the most compelling source of accomplishment for the Artist was financial. He raked in $30 million that year and did so at 70% profit margins—nearly double the standard take.

Other independent projects proved less successful. Anti-industrial vengeance still colored his vision, and he independently issued the two projects that, at least in name, Warner Bros. had refused to release: a triple-CD *Crystal Ball* set and a side project by the "N.P.G."

To bring the *Crystal Ball* package to market, the Artist created a new directselling operation, bringing his NPG retail phone service to the web as 1800newfunk.com. That operation proved to be disastrously incompetent, however, and it crumbled under the weight of 84,000 preorders. What fans received seven months after the promised arrival date was an unconsidered grab bag of outtakes from the vault. As payback on a 10-year-old grudge, the set presented several of the original 1987 tracks that had fallen to Warners' hatchet. Most all of them were already documented in the thousands of bootlegs in circulation, and the $60 package served as little more than the Artist's attempt at reclaiming some revenue from the bootleggers.

The more interesting work showed up on two accompanying bonus discs: *The Truth* CD and an album of orchestral music called *Kamasutra* that the Artist had composed and aired at his wedding. Both projects were lost in a pile of discs that never received an audience beyond his core fan base. Within this forest of songs, the Artist mourned his falling out from popular favor. On the naked *Truth*, he defied radio programmers with "DON'T PLAY ME," a depressed commentary on his lost commercial appeal. The music bared its gripping, unadulterated essence, and the lyric bared his soul. But poetically, it never got heard.

Five months after *Crystal Ball*, the Artist issued an album by the "N.P.G." called *Newpower Soul*—the name of his counter-cultural genre that emphasized live-instrument funk and soul. For this project, he enlisted the production and distribution services of BMG, but retained all the promotion duties himself (and kept all ownership control, of course). The most unusual aspect of the N.P.G. project was that the Artist himself served as the frontman, maximizing its chances for commercial success. In fact, he appeared solo on the cover under the banner of the "N.P.G.," momentarily sidestepping his symbol comedy.

The material on *Newpower Soul* wanted to get down and party, much like the Time, *Goldnigga* and *Exodus* before it; but few of the tracks had any musical interest, and the shallow intent left critics despairing the Artist's emotional vacancy and pedestrian funk.

Despite a burst of personal promotion—including a live interview on ABC's *Good Morning America*, performances on the *Today* show and *The Tonight Show*, a slick video single co-starring Rita Moreno and a short tour—the project died on arrival and disappeared without nary a glance from the general public.

The Artist was not impressing anyone with his independent models, and by the end of 1998, his public profile had virtually evaporated. In terms of commercial status, he had completed perhaps the steepest fall of any major artist—from the 1980s megastar whose shadow momentarily eclipsed Michael Jackson to a cult figure who struggled to be heard above the voices of N Sync and R. Kelly. The artist who held the longest consecutive string of yearly hits had only seen the top region of the charts once in the last six years. Once the darling of critics—a revolutionary genius—he was now largely ignored by the music press. The public shared the lack of interest in the tarnished star and his work, and Howard Stern aptly dubbed him "The Artist People Formerly Cared About."

TRACK 8: "UNDISPUTED"

The Artist understood that his ability to lead change depended on maintaining an active commercial presence. After the disappointment of *Emancipation* and *Newpower Soul*—on top of the scorched battlefield of three previous war-torn records—he still had a lot to prove to the world and to his old nemesis, Warner Bros.

His credibility crisis worsened in late 1998. First came the release of a planned comeback album for Chaka Khan. The Artist had goaded the "I Feel for You" star into following him across the Mason-Dixon line, even offering his lawyer, Londell McMillan, to help her out of her ties to Warner Bros. He then worked up an historic collaboration album—two greats partnering on Chaka's first solo effort in six years. The record—*Come 2 My House*—was written, performed and produced almost entirely by the Artist, and the inspiring material seemed certain to inspire critics. But the comeback project, issued by NPG Records and promoted by no one but themselves, went entirely unnoticed.

Then, a few months later, Warner Bros. stoked the Artist's ire by announcing the re-release of "1999" to usher in the year he'd made famous. Because the firm owned the master tapes, it was free to exploit his music.

The Artist shot back with a sly retort: releasing his own re-recording of the song, called "1999: The New Master." (He also pledged to re-record the rest of his back catalog but never followed through on the threat.) Warner Bros. got the last laugh however, as the original version climbed the charts while "The New Master" remained stuck in NPG Records oblivion.

Floundering to get his voice heard and his anti-industrial movement moving, the Artist posted an open letter to Madonna on his website, enlisting her support in revolutionizing the system. The letter went unanswered.

Nearing desperation in his quest for relevance, the Artist entertained getting back into bed with an industry label. In negotiations with the majors, the legendary Clive Davis at Arista offered a lucrative proposition of hit-making marketing. Davis had just engineered the multi-platinum comeback for Santana, with his *Supernatural* showcase of contemporary guests. Now, excited by the prospect of making success of another fallen genius, he gave the Artist an astounding package: an $11 million advance for a one-record deal and ownership of the master recordings. He convinced the Artist to sign and immediately began hyping the collaboration, promising the world—and the Artist—a massive hit.

For his part, the Artist brought a fully loaded cannon to Arista—a strong, accessible album designed to win him some airwaves. With heavy nods to contemporary R&B formats, *Rave Un2 the Joy Fantastic* was out to prove that the

Artist was an undisputed leader not to be ignored. On "UNDISPUTED," he reminded a new generation of artists that his achievements were still the high-water mark. "Hear me, feel me, love me," he insisted repeatedly as a heavy, syncopated rhythm pounded its fist on a table.

Borrowing a page from the *Supernatural* hat trick, he welcomed several high-profile guests onto his tracks—contemporary stars Sheryl Crow, Gwen Stefani of No Doubt and rapper Eve. He also partnered up with a couple of fellow freedom fighters, including Ani DiFranco, a successful independent on the alternative and college circuits. On "Undisputed," he joined with Chuck D—the former NWAer and an anti-industry warrior like himself—in the album's one political rally for artists' rights.

With a solid album and the firm commitment of both the Artist and Clive Davis, the great comeback machinery whirled into motion in late 1999—just in time for the millennium celebration for which he'd written the anthem.

The hype in advance of the release included news of a surprise guest producer, which in time, turned out to be none other than "Prince." Like the rest of his name games, it didn't go over too well.

Clive Davis tried to pump up the buzz with a pre-release event in New York City attended by 500 media and industry VIPs. He previewed the album tracks and touted the first single ("The Greatest Romance Ever Sold") as a certain chart topper. The Artist greased the machinery by performing live at these industry showcases, mimicking the programmer-friendly approach he'd used for *Diamonds and Pearls*. He also filmed the most polished video of his career (although he delivered it two months late) and created an entire mirror album of remixes and extended versions (*Rave In2 the Joy Fantastic*). He conducted another expansive round of interviews, including an appearance on *The View*, MTV's *Total Request Live* and an hour-long visit with CNN's Larry King. Three musician's journals—*Keyboard*, *Bass Player* and *Guitar Player* magazine—each featured a cover article proclaiming him a master in their respective fields. His all-out promotional effort peaked with a pay-per-view cable special on New Year's Eve 1999. A taped concert at Paisley Park, entitled *Rave Un2 the Year 2000*, featured performances by the Time, Lenny Kravitz and the Artist, who retired the song "1999" with a final rendition at midnight.

Even still—with all the elements at work on its behalf, including the dedication of a major label and fabled hitmaker—*Rave* failed to ignite. With fresh ass like the Backstreet Boys commanding the attention of teenagers and radio, the new single by the Artist ("The Greatest Romance") never accelerated after a few initial rotations, despite the servicing of a remix that featured heavy use of red-hot

Eve. Without the support of radio, the project fizzled on the launch pad, selling little more than his puny independent efforts of late. Any prospect of a relaunch disappeared when Clive Davis was ousted by Arista shortly thereafter.

With the failure of *Rave*, the only thing undisputed about the Artist's career was his commercial irrelevance. The mightiest of efforts couldn't overcome the years of image erosion caused by pompous preening, corporate warring and the lingering joke that was his name. His musical reinventions had ended a decade earlier and, along with it, the public's excitement for his work. With a seven-year absence from the charts, he'd become a non-entity in the world he once ruled.

TRACK 9: "CYBERSINGLE"

In the fallout of his rebound relationship with the music industry, the Artist redoubled his independent enterprise, and in the summer of 2000, he made several moves aimed at halting his career freefall and realigning himself with his core fans. The most significant was a down-to-earth, matter-of-fact press conference in New York, where he announced he was reclaiming his original name to mark the expiration of a final Warner contract and the cessation of his decade-long war.

The first single to mark the return of "Prince" was a free download— "CYBERSINGLE"—that revealed him in full sales mode, pitching his private Internet enterprise over a noisy rocker that still sounded more forced than free. The release promoted a new web domain (npgonlineltd.com) where he would occasionally delight his core fans with free music.

Prince also rewarded his loyalists by opening up his Paisley Park facility for a five-day "festival." The "Celebration" event, scheduled to coincide with Prince's birthday in June, turned into an annual affair that ran for three years (from 2000 to 2002) and included feature concerts by Prince, meet-and-greet dialogues with the star, and guest performances by the likes of Alicia Keys, Erykah Badu, Norah Jones and Common. He even treated the devotees, many of whom had traveled from around the world, to a free movie at the local suburban theater. In a surreal scene of fan-meets-artist intimacy, Prince's limo led a long caravan of rental cars to a private screening of *Minority Report*.

In 2001, Prince took his outreach program on the road, performing at small, intimate venues across the States. The "Hit and Run" shows reapplied his 1986 touring concept: quick in-and-out appearances announced only days in advance. They were bare-bones reviews of both his popular and eclectic gems, featuring a snappy new band that included Maceo Parker, James Brown's famous sax man. The tour was a chance to generate some public interest in the return of the prodigal

"Prince," restore his artistic luster, replenish his bank account and reconnect with his dedicated followers.

That same year, Prince inaugurated the next evolution of his independent, interactive business model. He created the NPG Music Club, an online subscription service which, for a $100 annual fee, delivered a folder of new downloads each month: freshly minted MP3s, "bootleg" MPEG videos and a one-hour radio show that mixed new material, protégé spotlights and replays of the classics. As the services expanded, members of the club received priority seating at his shows and exclusive invitations to pre-concert soundchecks during which Prince frequently chatted with the cozy collection of fans.

The model evolved again in 2003 with an upgraded graphical interface (npg-musicclub.com) that more fully met his interactive marketing vision. The site was a luxurious Paisley palace, similar to his 1994 CD-ROM, and it became his online community center. Traveling from room to room, users accessed a vault of classic samples, a theater of rotating video clips, his retail shop, discussion forums and a library of editorials. With a reduced subscription fee ($25), membership reportedly swelled to 400,000 people.

As the music industry in the new millennium continued to flat-line and fall deeper into a David and Goliath conflict with its artists, Prince's interactive alternative gained a measure of credibility. At the same time that several high-profile artists—including Alanis Morrisette, Tom Petty and Courtney Love—unionized to fight their unkind corporate conditions, many veteran acts with smaller but loyal fan bases turned to the Internet. Others like the Eagles, Jimmy Buffett and Natalie Merchant struck out on their own with private label businesses like Prince's.

Once again, His Royal Badness appeared to be at the forefront of a revolution.

TRACK 10: "THE EVERLASTING NOW"

In the years following his baby's death and the demise of his public position, Prince intensified his religious study and, in 1997, fell under the tutelage of Larry Graham—former Sly Stone bassist, his teenage idol and a practicing Jehovah's Witness. They'd met on the road during Prince's "Jam of the Year" tour and rapidly developed a deep musical and personal relationship. The 51-year-old Graham began collaborating with Prince in Bible study and in song and soon became an omnipresent figure in both his public and private lives. Throughout the late '90s, Larry regularly joined Prince's stage outfit, and Prince gave Larry free studio time at the Park to produce a comeback LP for his Graham Central Station (another under-promoted, invisible release on the NPG label). As their relationship deepened, Larry and his family relocated to Minneapolis to join the team at Paisley Park.

Larry's presence in Prince's life engendered another profound period of change. At the dawn of the new millennium, Prince posted a new tune called "One Song" on his website. It was prefaced by a six-minute speech that testified his new beliefs about God's construct for the universe.

The once salacious imp began an active pursuit of spiritual and physical purity. He continued to eat a strictly vegan diet (something he'd been doing for several years now) and dropped all curse words from his language. He instituted a no-swearing policy at the Park, and in performances, he cut the nasty tunes from his repertoire and altered lyrics that conflicted with his new religious perspectives. (Based on the Jehovahs' belief that Jesus died on a pole, he changed "The Cross" to "The Christ.")

By 2002, Prince had fully converted to a Jehovah's Witness and was making prayer visits to the local Kingdom Hall. The Minneapolis press reported that Prince and Larry were seen going door-to-door with religious leaflets in the neighborhoods adjoining Paisley Park. Naturally, as this news spread, it only served to exacerbate the public joke that the oddball recluse had become.

In the quietude of a marginalized career, Prince began to realize a more private paradigm of success. On New Year's Eve 2001, he married his second wife— Manuela Testolini, a diehard fan who'd been hired to manage his Love4OneAnother Charities—in a traditional Jehovah's Witness ceremony in Hawaii.

That same month, he released a new album that revealed a more contented spirit, even as it dwelled at the fringe. The record, the first since returning to "Prince," celebrated his new faith and his holy union with his wife. Amid the recent flurry of file transfers, it was the only actual plastic CD, a disc entitled *The Rainbow Children*. But once again, it took an off-the-beaten-path approach to market. Prince issued the first single ("The Work Part 1") not to radio, but as a free download on Napster. Members of his music club received the album through the Internet, and hard copies of the disc got spotty distribution in store through private deals with retailers.

The Rainbow Children was a religious concept album, and Prince didn't shy from his faith's evangelistic mission. Although it was marketed as "controversial," the heavy-handed spiritual dialogue—narrated between tracks by a "Tora Tora"-like preacher's voice—merely offended the critics. The ones who got past the self-righteousness, however, acclaimed the return of a more self-assured musicality. With another evolved band configuration, Prince embraced a live jazz style that rang truer to his artistry than the bombast of his production in the '90s. Like earlier creative highlights, the elation of spiritual rebirth and requited love inspired top-tier material.

The sense of joyful peace, composure and comfort in his personal direction was captured on "THE EVERLASTING NOW," a revelatory jam that celebrated the spiritual path of Sly Stone, another creative visionary who followed his divine muse into prayerful obscurity. Mocking his backward-looking detractors, Prince directed a musical party as vital and rapturously engaging as any he'd ever recorded.

The quiet triumph of *The Rainbow Children* preceded a line of offspring that reasserted his craftsmanship. *One Nite Alone* was the title of an acoustic piano album (sent exclusively to club subscribers) that cut to the marrow of his musicianship. It was a private recital, and many of the tracks contained deeply personal reflections on love lost and love found. It had been an emotional year for Prince—the joy of marriage had been tainted by the deaths of both his mother and father in the six months surrounding the wedding. The heartfelt musings of *One Nite Alone*, solo at the keyboard, captured his intimate, reflective mood.

One Nite Alone became the name of a 2002 theater tour that featured his new band's jazzy, stripped-down attire, lots of *Rainbow Children* material, and more of his distilled, purified, un-aging performance magic. The tour was later repackaged as a live box set (the first live-performance album of his long career) and as a video DVD.

All that was followed shortly thereafter by two jazz albums. The first—a free 2003 download given to club members—was called *Xpectation*, and it was a straightforward jazz instrumental LP notable only for its "X"-named song titles and interesting use of the violin. The second album, an actual CD entitled *N.E.W.S.*, tried to make a bit more impact and actually found its way into a handful of stores. This second, jazz-informed instrumental recording was cut live with his band in the studio and contained four fourteen-minute tracks of unstructured phrasings—the kind of self-indulgent whimsy his emancipation proclamations had promised.

Although these hermetic excursions of musicianship failed to generate any interest, they provided a refreshing deviation from a long and often awkward decade of career posturing. Though the impact of his music was still just a whisper, it finally spoke louder than his personal P.R.

TRACK 11: "MUSICOLOGY"

For many, the first public sighting of Prince in years came at the 2004 Grammy Awards. He kicked off the program with ultra-hot Beyoncé, doing a medley of *Purple Rain* hits that upstaged pop's reigning princess and stole the show. The next morning, his picture was splayed across the nation as the front-page feature of *USA Today*. Many of the writers who reviewed the show noted that the event's other big winner—OutKast's André 3000—was, in fact, the best Prince imitator in a generation.

The critical response to his reemergence at the Grammy's heralded a renaissance for Prince—the comeback many had long anticipated. After years of factory-made pop and the increasingly dull thud of hip-hop, the music world seemed ready to welcome back some buoyant originality and musicianship. And the 45-year-old Prince was ready to end his self-imposed exile.

It was an historic year for Prince. Not only was it the 20th anniversary of *Purple Rain*, but it was also the first year he was eligible for induction into the Rock and Roll Hall of Fame. And the music press promptly ushered him in. Turning what was typically a nostalgic memorial service into a glorious coming-out party, Prince used the March induction ceremony as another launching pad. For the second time in as many months, he stole the show at an industry showcase, breathing fresh energy into a medley of his '80s hits and upstaging Tom Petty, Steve Winwood and others during an all-star jam on George Harrison's "While My Guitar Gently Weeps." In a riveting, highly animated performance (*Rolling Stone* called it "devastating"), Prince shred a guitar solo for the history books, relegating the other veterans to invisible bystanders and mocking all those who'd doubted his preeminence.

That same month, he rolled out his most commercial album project in five years—a CD entitled *Musicology*, accompanied by a major arena tour of the same name. In another reinvention of his career—this time as elder statesman genius—music's messiah and his "MUSICOLOGY" message were out to save the world from mediocrity. On the promotional circuit, he championed "real music" and "real musicians" and decried the lip-synchers of the day. The lead single and its video release (sufficiently polished to secure a return to MTV rotation) uncorked some of James Brown's lost sorcery and reaffirmed the power of the old school.

Likewise, the new album was a lesson in Prince's time-honored pop magic, showcasing his organic originality with a more fun, focused and unfettered musicality. With spiritual politics momentarily swept to the side, it had a blend of craftsmanship and mainstream appeal that reviewers warmly embraced.

On tour, Prince produced a similar mix—channeling his greatest hits through a masterful live band while showcasing his own astonishing dexterity. On a bare-bones stage—set up "in the round" with four walkways that maximized the intimacy—Prince and his skilled ensemble produced sensational jams, punctuated by instrumental solos and old-school horns. The highlight was an acoustic guitar set performed alone by Prince.

Overnight, His Royal Badness seemed to re-enliven an industry demoralized by corporate collapse, shallow, plastic pop and the sorry affairs of Brother and Sister Jackson. And the critical establishment rushed to Prince's corner. Any over-exposure problems in the '90s had been corrected by a 10-year absence, and many critics who'd dismissed him as irrelevant now celebrated Prince's return. One major publication after another pronounced, "Prince is back." *Entertainment Weekly* and *Rolling Stone* gave his comeback the cover, and *Rolling Stone* listed him as one of the 50 "Immortals" of rock.

Prince paved the way for his resurgence with charming appearances on the *Jay Leno* and *Ellen DeGeneres* shows that made it all too easy to like him again. On PBS's *The Tavis Smiley Show*, he chatted at length—and with great humility—about his long career, then wowed fans with a moving acoustic performance backed by surprise guest Wendy Melvoin.

With all the hype surrounding it, the 2004 tour took off like a rocket, with widespread sellouts and multiple big-city dates (five arena shows in L.A. and six in the New York area). He'd generated some additional interest by declaring that the concerts would be a farewell tour for his '80s hits. He then staged a thrilling kickoff on March 29th—a command performance before a record-breaking crowd at Los Angeles' Staples Center, beamed live into movie theaters in 43 cities. The show opened with a video of the ecstatic speech given by Alicia Keys—another one of the contemporary protégés that suddenly seemed to pop up everywhere—at his induction into the Rock and Roll Hall of Fame.

The zealous reaction from the L.A. crowd confirmed his victory.

That same day, Prince made several marketing maneuvers that showed him to be a relentless innovator, independently creating new models for the business of music. At the L.A. show—and with each subsequent stop—he gave away copies of his new CD to all the concertgoers. The cost of the record was built into the ticket price, and with this simple act, Prince generated a whole new class of "album sales"—hundreds of thousands of units moved at full profit—while creating extensive viral buzz for his official, in-store release. The new approach forced Nielsen SoundScan to rethink its accounting principles, and *Billboard's* decision to include the "giveaways" in Prince's rankings rocked the industry.

On the first day of the tour, the online NPG Music Club also launched its own iTunes-like download store—a first-of-its-kind retail operation for an independent star. The new *Musicology* CD was made available on the site, as was some of his previous online output (newly reconfigured as albums under the titles *The Slaughterhouse* and *Chocolate Invasion*).

The *Musicology* CD also received a more conventional push, courtesy of another one of Prince's promotion and distribution deals with a major label—this time with Sony's Columbia Records. The firm's high-profile marketing effort included an unprecedented simulcast TV special, broadcast on all five of the MTV, VH-1 and BET-affiliated channels. The primetime event featured live concert footage from New York's Webster Hall—with an unplugged guitar set that quaintly showcased his skills.

With all that working on its behalf, a Prince album returned to the upper reaches of the charts (debuting at #3) for the first time in over a decade.

Prince had finally transformed his independent enterprise into mainstream success.

The impact of the not so little phenomenon from Minneapolis was felt once more, and as the revival continued, His Purple Highness seemed to regain his rightful throne. Prince was, once again, the self-made King.

Epilogue

No other artist has ever succeeded so greatly—and often fallen so dramatically—on the libertarian ideal of creativity. Nor has anyone ever generated such mammoth activity in the quest. He's been an explosion of titanic drive and incendiary talent that produced some of the most spectacular fireworks in pop history, even if ashes of egotism sometimes ruined the view.

Nowhere in the rock n' roll myth have such troubled beginnings created such colossal ambition. Putting on a costume he would never take off, he turned himself into the most complete musical virtuoso of all time and an unrivalled master of the stage. He's one of the very few artists who truly earned the mantle of "genius."

The responsibility of these achievements was never lost on Prince, who used his medium to mount a divine crusade. Beneath all the shock value and laughable peculiarities was an essential struggle of the human spirit—a journey of conflict between primal smallness and the pursuit of higher being. Booming statements from a very quiet man.

A consummate artist, he insisted on complete creative liberty—freedom from classification, freedom from repression, even freedom from his own past if it got it the way. He was undaunted in his sense of personal style and never lost his thirst for the daring. Many artists preached the religion of creative muse; Prince actually practiced it. He's rewritten the book on artistic enterprise and become the poster child for an industrial revolution. He's redefined the meaning of prolific, even as his career often drowned in his own self-absorbed genius.

In the sheer breadth of his artistic force, his life has been a celebration of creation.

BIBLIOGRAPHY

Bream, Jon, *Prince: Inside the Purple Reign*, Macmillan Publishing Company, 1984

Bull, Bart, "Black Narcissus," *Spin*, Vol. 2, Number 4, July 1986

Controversy magazine, Issues 22-43, 1990-1993

Duffy, John, *Prince: An Illustrated Biography*, Omnibus Press, 1992

Ehrlich, Dimitri, "Portrait of The Artist as a Free Man," *Notorious*, Issue 4, November/December 1999

Feldman, Jim, *Prince*, Ballantine Books, 1984

Hahn, Alex, *Possessed: The Rise and Fall of Prince*, Billboard Books, 2003

Hill, David, *Prince: A Pop Life*, Harmony Books, 1989

Hoskyns, Barney, *Prince: Imp of the Perverse*, Virgin, 1988

Infantry, Ashante, "Return of the Purple Reign," *Toronto Star*, April 18, 2004

Jones, Liz, *Purple Reign: The Artist Formerly Known as Prince*, Birch Lane Press, 1998

Karlen, Neal, "The Prince of Paisley Park," *Rolling Stone*, Issue 456, September 12, 1985

Nilsen, Per, *DanceMusicSexRomance—Prince: The First Decade*, Firefly Publishing, 1999

Perry, Steve, "Prince: The King of 'Em All," *Musician*, Number 121, November 1988

Poulson-Bryant, Scott, "Fresh Prince," *Spin*, Vol. 7, Number 6, September 1991

Rowland, Mark and Margy Rochlin, *Prince: His Story in Words and Pictures*, Critics Choice, 1985

Sutcliffe, Phil, "The Artist Formerly Known as Successful," *Q*, September 1998

Touré, "The Artist," *Icon*, October 1998

Uptown, *Days of Wild*, 2000
Uptown magazine, Issues 1-27, 1991-1997

ABOUT THE AUTHOR

Matthew Carcieri has followed Prince's career for over 20 years. He's a musician, copywriter and marketing professional whose articles have appeared in newspapers and newsletter publications. He lives 782 miles southeast of Minneapolis.

0-595-32012-0

Printed in the United Kingdom
by Lightning Source UK Ltd.
120425UK00003B/408